To my good friend
Rid

allays

Fred S. Maples

~~10/6/19~~

12/1/19

DESTINED TO BE A
SUBMARINER

DESTINED TO BE A
SUBMARINER

FRED F. MAPHIS

Library of Congress Control Number:		2017917435
ISBN:	Hardcover	978-1-5434-6525-9
	Softcover	978-1-5434-6526-6
	eBook	978-1-5434-6527-3

Print information available on the last page.

Rev. date: 01/03/2018

To order additional copies of this book, contact:
Xlibris
1-888-795-4274
www.Xlibris.com
Orders@Xlibris.com
768722

Contents

The Beginning

It all started during the winter of 1944 in war-torn Germany. In the city of Liegnitz on the twenty-eighth of February at about 22:00, I was born. At the time, my mother was alone, although living with her father and sisters. Her husband, my father, was presumed dead. He had been a crew member of a German submarine that had been lost at sea. A submarine lost at sea has little chance of any survivors.

My mother's father, my grandfather, told Mom that she, her baby (me), and her sisters should try to get to southwestern Germany before the Russians arrive. Liegnitz was in far eastern Germany, in what is now Poland. Her father could see the handwriting on the wall. He realized Germany was losing the war and the Russians would most likely control eastern Germany. Fearing the Russian soldiers would commit atrocities against the civilian population, my grandfather wanted Mom, me, and her sisters to be in a much safer place.

Traveling through war-ravaged Germany was very traumatic for Mom and her sisters. They had to evade Russian soldiers, brave air raids, and even endure being strafed by US aircraft while riding on a train. All the while, Mom was trying to take good care of me.

After a few days, they made it to the town of Erding in the south of Germany. There we stayed with Mama Gross, a close family relative. Erding was just south of Munchen (Munich). This ensured that we would be in an area controlled by the Americans. Also, in the Munich area, Mom had a better chance of finding work.

During this time, I became gravely ill, and Mom had extreme difficulty obtaining nutritious food and needed medication for me. Nevertheless, she devoted all her energy and resources trying to obtain what was needed to keep me healthy.

On an afternoon during the winter of 1946, while shopping, Mom was involved in a traffic accident. The streetcar she was riding was hit by a US Army half-track. Fortunately, no one was seriously hurt. However, the German officials and military police had to sort out what had happened. This took some time, allowing a young Sgt. Robert W. Maphis, riding as a passenger in the half-track, to notice Mom. He was infatuated by her. During the weeks and months following the accident, Sergeant Maphis began seeing Mom quite often.

Sgt. Maphis was assigned to the Munich area as a member of the American occupation force. This proved to be a godsend for me. Sgt. Maphis exploited the black market and any other means at his disposal to bring medications and various foods, fruits, and vegetables for Mom and me when he could come for visits. After a few months, I became well, while Mom and Sgt. Maphis fell in love and planned their wedding.

It should be noted that before Sgt. Maphis had advanced to the grade of sergeant, he had been a tail gunner in a B-17 bomber aircraft nicknamed the Flying Fortress. He had made numerous bombing missions over Germany. On several of these bombing missions, he lost many friends and comrades to both enemy aircraft gunfire and flak from ground fire. This explained Sgt. Maphis's attitude and action toward my real father.

B-17 Flying Fortress, in which Sgt. Maphis
had been a Tail Gunner

To the surprise of all, my real father had not died at sea. Yes, his submarine had been lost, but he and a few others had escaped drowning and were captured. They spent the remainder of the war in a prison camp. It was almost 1947 before the repatriation of all prisoners was complete. By this time, Mom and Sgt. Maphis were very much in love and married. Therefore, when my real father appeared, my mother and stepfather's first wedding had to be annulled, and Mom had to get a divorce from her first marriage to my real father. This made Sgt. Maphis very upset to the point that he wanted to kill my real father. With the bombing missions still haunting him, my stepfather viewed my real father as the enemy and a threat to his marriage to Mom. After the situation calmed down, Sgt. Maphis and Mom were remarried on the twenty-eighth of August 1948.

Sergeant Maphis and Mom's Marriage
in Munich on 8/28/1948

Additionally, the army air corps improved the situation by transferring Sgt. Maphis to Andrews Air Base, outside Washington, DC. Mom and I followed him a month or so later.

Me, Mom, and Sergeant Maphis in late 1948

Even to this day, I have faint memories of the trip to the United States. Mom and I came to the United States on a transport ship. I remember the man walking down the passageways with a small xylophone playing a little tune when it was mealtime. I also remember being in our cabin during a storm and hearing dishes and such crashing to the floor. It seems our cabin was next to the kitchen.

When we arrived in the United States, we lived in a trailer in a trailer court not far from Andrews Air Force Base. I was about six years old when I almost burned the entire trailer down. You see, Dad had built a small porch for the trailer and had what were the forerunners of lawn chairs and a table on it. One day there were some cardboard boxes left on the porch, and I was playing with matches. Needless to say, the boxes caught fire; the porch would have caught fire had the neighbor not seen what was happening and put out the fire with a garden hose. Boy! Did I get a spanking! Also, during this time, I learned to call Sergeant Maphis, my stepfather, daddy.

We lived in Washington, DC, about two years. Here, Mom became Americanized, and I started school. Because I was not able to speak English, the narrow-minded school teacher told my mother to only speak English at home. My mother was frightened of the teacher and only spoke English as best she could. This was very unfortunate. I learned to speak English quickly, but I forgot all my German, save a few words. Also, my love for Daddy, my stepfather, began to blossom. To this day, I only have fond memories and love for my stepfather. I will always consider him my father.

During my childhood, we moved very often, as Daddy remained in the army air corps, which later became the US Air Force. After Andrews Air Base, we moved to England for a three-year assignment. It was in England in 1953 that my sister Roberta was born. I have very little memories of England. We lived in a row house and had a coal-burning fireplace for heat. From England, Dad was transferred to Castle Air Force Base in Atwater, California.

We were at Castle AFB for almost five years. Dad bought a small three-bedroom, one-bath home on Elm Street. The street number was 445. Isn't it strange how one remembers little things like that?

Our house on 445 Elm Ave.

There, I attended school from the fourth grade through the eighth grade. While in Atwater, my brother Robert and my baby sister Darlene were born. Actually, Darlene was born in Chowchilla. You see, my dad loved to make music with others he would find that played instruments. Being a *big* fan of country/Western music, Dad always formed a country and Western band everywhere he was stationed. Besides enjoying playing music, he enjoyed the extra money it would bring in. Mom was pregnant with Darlene and was with Dad in Chowchilla, California, while he was playing a gig. Before the night was over, Mom went into labor.

Additionally, while in Atwater, in 1956 I became a United States citizen. Mom, Dad and I all went to the Merced, CA. county court house, where I took my oath of allegiance. As a part of naturalization I took Maphis as my sur name.

I made many school friends while in Atwater. Like most grade-school students, many of the kids would retell stories about the war (World War II) that their fathers had told them. This prompted me to ask my dad to tell me some war stories. Finally, after much prodding and pestering, my dad told me about one of his bombing missions. I think I will always remember the gist of this story. First of all, my father went into a great deal of detail and was very graphic. Additionally, I could see it pained him to relive the experience. On this particular mission, he and the pilot were the only ones to make it back alive. They encountered very heavy flak, and the plane was nearly torn apart. The flak was successful in killing all but the captain and my dad. He explained how he and the pilot tried to save the lives of their crewmates. Using everything in the first aid kit, they tried to bandage their wounds and tried to stop the bleeding, only to be sorrowed by their condition. The heavy flak literally tore their bodies apart. Dad was almost brought to tears reliving this experience. I never again asked him to tell me another story.

Getting back to my school years and friends, one friend in particular was Keith Parker. His house was less than a five-minute walk from our house. We would walk to and from school together almost every day. Speaking of walking to and from school reminds me of snitching pomegranates. On our trek home we would pass a corner house with a large pomegranate tree near the fence. Either Keith or I would climb the fence and grab two pomegranates and eat them the rest of the way home. We did this almost the entire time there was pomegranates on the tree. Keith and I became the best of friends. I still remember building a not-so-good tree house in a large cottonwood tree next to his driveway. It is a wonder we didn't fall out and seriously hurt ourselves. The two of us and another friend, David Bettis, all entered the navy and went to boot camp together.

During the summer, before my freshman year, my dad was transferred to Riverside, CA. In Riverside, during the summer, I worked at the base commissary as a grocery sacker on the morning shift. I would get off work about 13:30 and go to the riding stables about three times a week. During this time, I really learned to enjoy horseback riding.

On the Goose

Before my freshman year was over, my dad was transferred to Goose Air Force Base in Goose Bay, Labrador. Before going further, let me relate a little more about my childhood. While I was growing up, Dad always had a boat. At the beginning, it was just a small boat, a little bigger than a rowboat. We would go fishing quite often. However, on the Goose, Dad bought a much bigger boat. During the summer months, Dad, a couple of his friends, and I would go almost into Lake Melville, a saltwater tidal extension of the Hamilton Inlet. The Hamilton Inlet, with Lake Melville, is the largest estuary on the Labrador coast. In reality, the Hamilton Inlet is a very large fjord. The waters at times could become as treacherous as the open ocean in a violent storm. The boat Dad bought was a pretty good size. She was about forty feet long, looked like an ark, could handle almost any type of weather, sleep six comfortably, and had a full galley. Most of the time, we would go out on overnight fishing trips. However, on occasion, we would stay out for three or four days. It was great fishing and being with Dad and his friends. I really enjoyed those fishing trips. These wonderful memories may have been another reason for my affinity to join the navy!

Aerial view of Goose Air Force Base

During the winter months, the boat was taken out of the water and put on blocks. On nice days, I would help Dad clean the bottom of the boat and insure her seaworthiness. Speaking of winter, I remember Dad taking me ice fishing. On my first trip, I was in for a big surprise. I couldn't believe my eyes! There was an actual village of small cabins on the ice, each being used for ice fishing. The first time I went into the cabin, it blew my mind. The cabin was very warm, with chairs all around a large hole in the ice. There was even a little cabinet to hold fishing tackle and even food. As the cabin was very warm, I was afraid we would melt through the ice and end up in the bay! Dad assured me the ice was about two feet thick and we would not melt through. It was great fun!

Another thing I vividly remember about Goose Bay is the northern lights (the aurora borealis). Keep in mind, Goose

Bay is less than a thousand miles from the Arctic Circle, allowing good viewing of the northern lights. The aurora is the result of charged particles from the sun striking atoms and exciting the electrons in our atmosphere. This causes the vivid colors to ripple through the night sky. The aurora borealis has been seen as far south as Washington, DC. As for me, I am convinced the aurora is the result of God putting on a beautiful display of colored lights throughout the heavens. There on the Goose, I was able to see and truly enjoy the most spectacular light shows on earth. These were some of the most beautiful events I had ever seen!

I attended my sophomore and junior year of high school while Dad was stationed on Goose Bay. During my sophomore and junior year of high school, I worked as a grocery sacker after school at the base commissary. I also worked at the base Teen Town as a soda jerk during the summers on Fridays or Saturdays. The summer between my sophomore and junior years of high school, I worked part-time washing dishes and as a cleanup person at the enlisted men's club. I became friends with the cook, and he allowed me to help cook simple meals. This proved to be rather rewarding, as I learned to cook simple meals, hamburgers, and pizzas. Unfortunately, during this time, I was not a very good student. You see, I discovered girls! Subsequently, I spent almost all my time working to make the necessary money to chase girls instead of paying attention to my schoolwork.

Goose Air Force Base Dependent School

Had we stayed on the Goose, I would not have become a senior, as I did not have enough credits. Therefore, the Goose Air Base dependent school decided to let the new school I would be attending make the decision whether I would be a senior.

Fortunately, Dad was transferred back to Castle AFB in Atwater, CA. There the Atwater High School officials waived a few credits and allowed me to make up for other needed credits by taking a correspondence course and taking an extra class during the first semester. This was all needed for me to be a senior. I think I was the only senior that was attending school nine hours a day. The good thing was, it allowed me to graduate with most of the same students with whom I had gone to elementary school during fourth through eighth grade.

Atwater High School

During the summer, before entering my senior year, I worked a number of jobs to get the spending money I wanted. My parents were not rich! Although we did have adequate food and a small three-bedroom, one-bath home, my parents were not raising only me; I had two sisters and a brother. We all needed clothing, food, school supplies, and everything else associated with raising children. They were unable to give me personal spending money to go on dates or other personal things I wanted to do or have. Therefore, I had to find jobs and work. These jobs included cutting grapes, knocking and racking almonds, swamping peaches, and picking cotton.

Cutting grapes allows one to enjoy time with bees; grapes are sweet and have pollen. Besides the bees, while trying to cut in a hurry to make more money, you have the opportunity to cut your fingers. *Not fun!* Picking cotton is horrible! Cotton plants have long spines that stab you while you're reaching for the cotton ball. After four hours of picking, I made a whopping fifty cents. Boy, that is only about twelve cents an hour. Even for 1961, that was terrible! Nevertheless, if I wanted spending money, I had to work for it. Most of the time, I would mow grass. I would push the lawn mower up and down the streets, looking for homes that needed their grass mowed. This usually provided me with fifteen to twenty dollars a week. This was more than enough to take a girl to the movies and pay my share of the insurance on the family car. You see, I could not afford a car, so in order to use the car, I had to pay the extra cost for the insurance on me.

It was during my senior year of high school that the course was set for my adult life. At the beginning of 1962, I saw the movie **Run Silent, Run Deep** with Clark Cable and Burt Lancaster. This movie motivated me to want to join the navy and be a submariner. At that time, I didn't care what I did, as long as I could do it on a submarine. So during spring break, Keith Parker, David Bettis, and I went to Fresno, California, and did all the preliminary paperwork necessary for us to join the navy after high school graduation. Prior to my entering the navy, Dad told me many things about the military. First and foremost was to keep my mouth shut and do what I was told. The only exception was when I knew for sure I was one hundred percent right.

My senior picture

Off to Boot Camp and Initial Training

High school graduation was on June 6, 1962. By the 13th of June, I was in navy boot camp. It was *not* exactly what I expected. We were rousted out of bed about 04:30 every morning, except for Sunday. On Sundays, we were allowed to rest a little longer and to sleep in until about 05:30. We were always in a hurry, just to end up waiting. The phrase "hurry up and wait" seems to be synonymous with all the military services. I began to look forward to attending a training class of some type. This way, I could at least sit and rest while listening to lectures and taking notes. There was one week of basic training I remember rather vividly. It was the firefighting week. To be sure, my first fire was extremely frightening. I thought for sure I would die.

It was my first fire, a compartment fire, and I still vividly remember it. I was the number 4 man on the hose. The compartment became so full of thick smoke and extremely *hot* I felt certain we were all going to die. I actually thought the instructor and the number 1 and 2 men were either dead or overcome by smoke. I told the number 3 man to check and see if the nozzleman and instructor were still alive. Finally, the instructor told the nozzleman to turn on the water, and we began to fight the fire. Once we started fighting the fire, it took less than fifteen minutes, and the fire was out. I soon realized it is possible to put out large fires with teamwork and good training.

During the first weeks or so of basic training, I remember having to take a very large number of many different types of tests—basic battery tests. (Note: The navy and the military have realized it is best to give these tests before basic training.) Of all the basic battery tests I had taken, my best score was on the sonar hearing test. Having made the minimum score required for being in electronics and, at that time, having excellent hearing, I was encouraged to become a sonarman. I told the classifier that as long as sonarmen were on submarines, I would do it. Needless to say, the sonar rate is very important on submarines.

While in boot camp, I was made what we called a second-class marlin spike—actually a squad leader—and was in charge of a squad of about ten men. Why I was chosen for this task baffles me. However, it had its advantages. All my watches were in an office with plenty of coffee and time to write letters. This was very gratifying, especially during the middle of the night and when it was raining.

Me and David Bettis in boot camp

One more thing about boot camp that may be of interest: In the early sixties, we had to wash our own clothes by hand. There were big concrete tables able to accommodate about twenty sailors at a time, to be used when washing our underclothes and regular work clothes. For me, this wasn't a problem. However, for a friend of mine, the inspections were a real problem. He would get nailed almost every time. You see, we had a personnel inspection every morning, except for Sundays. At inspection, we had to grab our undershirt with our thumb in such a way as to show the inspector the seam where the main body of the shirt is sewn to the collar. This part of an undershirt is the easiest part to get dirty. My friend was not very accomplished at getting that part of his shirt nice and white, but he was excellent at spit shining his shoes. So, we agreed to let me wash his undershirts and he would shine my shoes. From then on, we both passed inspection with flying colors!

I graduated boot camp with the grade of seaman apprentice (E-2). After boot, I was sent to Naval Air Station Miramar just outside San Diego for about four months. It seems Miramar was in need of a compartment cleaner and mess cook (a galley worker). Go figure! Oh well, it didn't hurt me, and for the most part, it was okay duty. While at the bus station, awaiting the bus to NAS Miramar, I went to the snack bar to have a cup of coffee and a bite to eat. I sat next to a slick sleeve, second class. That is a person that made second-class petty officer (E-5) in less than four years. This is a very rare accomplishment. Naturally, I thought he was a motivated sailor being transferred to his next duty station. To my amazement, he was just honorably discharged and on his way home. I asked him, if he didn't like the navy, why did he work so hard to get advanced? He looked me straight in the eye and said, "Just because I don't like this outfit doesn't mean I'm stupid. The more rank you make, the more money you make and the less shitty details you have to perform." That really made a lasting impression on me because it really made a lot of sense!

At NAS Miramar, I was line captain of the chief petty officer's mess line in the dining hall for about two and a half months. As line captain, I was off every other day at about 14:00. This allowed me plenty of time to go to the Miramar riding stables and ride for about three to five hours every other day. I really enjoyed riding out in the hills and trying to be one with nature. It was very peaceful and relaxing, and it allowed me time to think. You must remember, in the early sixties, Miramar was out in the country and rolling hills, about thirty miles northwest of San Diego. It was an uninhabited area. One could ride for hours and never go over the same place twice. I wish I had had the foresight to have bought a few acres of land back then. Boy! I would be sitting pretty now! That entire area was fully developed into several cities.

From NAS Miramar, I went on to submarine sonar "A" school, also located in San Diego. Before my class was to start, I contracted bronchial pneumonia and was sent to Balboa Naval Hospital. It was there I exercised one of the lessons my father taught me. It was very early in the morning when the nurse woke me up. She said my sheets had to be replaced because my extreme sweating had made the entire bed very wet. So, I sat in the chair next to the bed and waited for her to make the bed. About twenty minutes later, I had fallen asleep in the chair, the nurse woke me up and told me to make the bed. I looked at her with some bewilderment and told her to make it! Remember, I was only a seaman apprentice (E-2). She became indignant and said she was a lieutenant and I was a seaman. I calmly told her she was a nurse and I was a very sick patient. She made the bed; however, about an hour or so later, she came back and drew blood.

Being at the hospital did provide some added training and benefit. Although the medical treatment was good, the administrative capacity was lacking. I stayed at the hospital after recovering from my illness for about four weeks, doing what was referred to as rehab. I was assigned to work in TB x-ray. This was an interesting assignment! I became acquainted with developing x-rays and even a little familiar with the basics of reading some of the x-rays. Additionally, an experimental operating room that was used for animals was just down the hall. This operating room was used to check out new procedures and experiments. I was allowed to observe the operations and procedures that were being developed. This was very interesting.

However, the downside was having missed my sonar school class start date. It was only because I wanted more liberty (time off) that I became anxious to get back to the sonar school. At the hospital, we were on "port and starboard" duty sections (two sections). This only gave me time off every other day and every other weekend. At sonar school, we were on six-section duty. Six-section duty would give me five days off in every six. Therefore, I set out to find the reason I was being kept from being sent back to school. The outcome was quite simple. It seems the doctor was waiting on paperwork from administration, and administration was waiting on paperwork from the doctor. There was an easy solution. I walked the necessary forms between the doctor and admin, and I was sent back to sonar school that very day.

A few days later, I entered the next submarine sonar class "A" school. By the afternoon of the first day of training, I discovered how important high school was. We were doing math I didn't know existed. Additionally, I was introduced to physics, electronics, and chemistry. By the end of the first week, I was completely *lost*! But there was a place for me and the others that were lost. It was called mandatory night school and no liberty. Additionally, to my good fortune, a sympathetic chief took a liking to me. Why, I will never know. Nevertheless, I will remember this chief to my dying day. His name was Chief Keary. He helped me make it through the entire twenty weeks of training. However, I was in mandatory night school for sixteen of the twenty weeks. There was only enough time to spend an hour or so at the gym before evening meal and then night school. This did allow me to get in shape and tone up. By the end of sonar "A" school, I was in the best shape of my life. During this time, I had no idea Chief Keary would again save my bacon.

Before completing "A" school, I was advanced to seaman (E-3). This also proved to have an obstacle not to my liking. Before I could take the seaman test, I had to perform "practical factors," which included knot tying. Boy! What a hassle! I had trouble tying my shoes. It took three tries before I got through the knot-tying test. This had to be done with a little trickery. I practiced three difficult knots until I became proficient. Then I went with a couple of other sailors before the boatswain's mate. There we were all asked to tie knots one at a time. Naturally, we started with easy knots and progressed to the more difficult. Each time one of the group was unable to tie a difficult knot I had learned, I told the boatswain I could do it. This went on for two of the three difficult knots I had learned. The "boats" was tired of me showing off, so he signed my card. I passed and was told to leave. Had I been asked to tie anything else, I would have been screwed. You know what they say: "No balls, no blue chips!" Put another way, sometimes a little deception is in order.

On my way to my next assignment, I had a few days' delay in route to stop by Mom and Dad's for a very short visit. While there, I helped one of Dad's friends move into a new house. After each day of the two days moving furniture, Dad's friend would take us to dinner at a restaurant. When he learned I was headed for New London, Connecticut, he gave me ten dollars and said I should go to a very nice restaurant and have a one- to one-and-a-half-pound Maine lobster. Remember, this was the sixties, and ten dollars was more than enough money for a lobster.

To Submarine School and My First Boat

So, after completing sonar "A" school, I was transferred to New London, Connecticut, to the submarine base in Groton. Many of us referred to the base as Rotten Groton. There I would find myself in mandatory night school again. Chief Keary used to always tell me I was "thick as shit and light as air." A couple of the sub school instructors told me the only reason I was not washed out was because I was classified as a submarine sonarman striker (apprentice). Sonar, at that time, was a very critical rate, and sonar technicians were in short supply on submarines. Therefore, it was another eight-week period with very little liberty. The only liberty I really remember is going with a couple of other mates to have the Maine lobster dinner I was told to have. To my surprise, I found I did not like lobster and still don't to this day.

During the entire training, the one thing I will never forget is mastering the "blow and go" escape training. During that phase of training, I felt *sure* I was going to meet my Maker! After we all were given the instructions, illustrations, and explanations, we were taken to the escape training tank. This was a very intimidating one-hundred-foot tower filled with water. There was a lock at the hundred-foot level and the fifty-foot level. In groups of four, we were taken to the fifty-foot level lock. With the four of us and the instructor in the lock, it was flooded and pressurized, and the door allowing entrance to the tank was opened. One at a time, we were told to take a deep breath, step into the tank, and "blow and go" to the surface. I was the third to leave the lock. Not having a clue what had happened to the other two sailors that left before me, the instructor told me to go. I was so scared I told the instructor I did not want to go. He told me to just remember what I had been taught and it would be all right. *Sure*, I was going to be able to continually "blow" from fifty feet below the surface all the way to the top. *Right!* I was *so* scared I *begged* the instructor to let me out. He assured me I would not drown and encouraged me to go for it. So I took a deep breath and left the lock for the surface. Blowing all the way, my life vest carried to the surface, and I bobbed out of the water like a cork. When the doctor, who was observing, asked me how I felt, all I could say was **"I'm alive, I'm alive!"** Now that I knew I could do it, I was ready for my second ascent. Each student had to make two ascents. During the second ascent, I was relaxed and even showed off a little by turning around to see all the paintings on the side of the tank. There were paintings of mermaids, fish, and the like all around the tank.

Escape training tank
Official Photograph, U. S. Navy

Near the end of sub school, I was assigned orders to the nuclear attack submarine, USS *Queenfish* SSN 651, requiring a secret clearance. This proved to be more difficult than I thought it would be. I had to call Mom and gather information about all her family members. After I had filled out all the forms for the background check and upon learning of all the relatives I had behind the Iron Curtain and in East Germany, my orders were canceled. This left me concerned whether I would be able to go on submarines. Little did I know that it was a blessing in disguise. I was given orders to a conventional submarine (a modified World War II diesel boat) stationed in Pearl Harbor, Hawaii.

Before going to Hawaii, I went home (on leave) to visit Mom and Dad. It was a good feeling to visit home and see the change in the way my parents talked to and treated me. They were very proud of me. However, my mother was very apprehensive of me being a submariner. She remembered getting word that my real father had been lost at sea. It was then that I learned that my real father had been a submariner. *Boy!* This was really a shock to me. All the while I was growing up, I had believed my real father was a ground pounder (infantry) in the German army. Maybe this was why I was so infatuated with wanting to be a submariner. ***For sure, it was truly my destiny!***

My first boat was the USS *Greenfish* (SS 351), stationed at Pearl Harbor, Hawaii. She was a GUPPY 3A—basically, a World War II submarine that had been retrofitted with advanced electronics, underwater capabilities, and slightly better living conditions (very slightly). However, she was my first boat and will always have a special meaning to me. Not only did I earn my Dolphins, the designator showing I was qualified in submarines, but I also met the love of my life while stationed on *Greenfish*.

Aerial view of SUBASE Pearl Harbor

I was on *Greenfish* for just about a year, arriving in Hawaii first at NAS Barbers Point in late September of 1963. I couldn't believe it! The weather was gorgeous; the ocean was crystal clear, turquoise in color, and warm. After a few days, I was provided with transportation and reported aboard *Greenfish*. It didn't take long to fit in—that is, be a part of the crew. I understood I was a *nothing* until I became qualified. Put another way, I was lower than whale shit. However, if you were up or ahead of the qualification schedule, things were pretty good. I had been assigned to the sonar gang and began working with the leading sonarman immediately. Those first few months aboard *Greenfish*, we performed weekly operations in and around Hawaiian waters, most of the time on training operations with surface vessels, mainly destroyers playing hide-and-seek. This provided me with ample time to learn my job as a sonarman and work on submarine qualifications. Additionally, we were informed the boat was going to go into the shipyard for a major overhaul and all the non-quals (those of us not qualified) should work to complete all at-sea qualifications.

Being only a seaman (E-3), I was assigned a cleaning station, as were all the members of the crew below E-6. Lucky me, my cleaning station was the after-battery head. For you civilians, that was the toilet in the after-battery compartment (the third compartment from the bow). On *Greenfish*, the after-battery was where the galley was located and about 60 percent of the crew's berthing. Needless to say, that particular head (bathroom) was used more than any other and was always in need of cleaning. After much thought and contemplation, I had an idea that, I believed, would help keep the head clean. As almost everything in the head is either stainless steel or brass, I decided not only to clean extremely well but to polish everything also! The sink and toilet bowl were so shiny you could see your reflection in them. All the piping and fixtures were also able to produce your reflection. With the head so exceptionally clean, crew members started cleaning up after themselves. It seems the crew members didn't want the next person waiting to use the head to know they were the ones to dirty it up! This made my job so much easier and made the crew members feel good about having a clean bathroom to use in which to do their business! This also taught me an important lesson: Do it right the first time, and it will go much better the next time.

USS *Greenfish SS 351*

Working on my qualifications was not as difficult as I thought it was going to be. After all the trouble I had in submarine school, I was a bit apprehensive as to my ability to learn all the ship's systems. Yet being able to see, touch, and operate the systems put it all into perspective. In sub school, it was almost all in the classroom, with very little hands-on operating and controlling the ship's systems. Now on the boat, not only could I see all the actual systems, but I could also operate them and control them. For example, as a submariner, you had to be able to make water; help operate the main engines; control the depth; pump water to and from the various tanks to maintain list/ballast, and also to and from the sea; operate the electric motors; etc. Actually, performing all these tasks made it easy for me to remember and understand the operating principles of a submarine.

Learning to make fresh water from salt water proved to be very easy. You see, I was accused of wasting water because I had filled the sink with water several times to give myself a washcloth bath. The leading torpedo man said I was wasting water! I was using water that was needed for the ship's batteries. I told him I wanted to be clean. He said we would be in port in a few days and I should have waited to shower in port. As a punishment, I was given a "still" (evaporator) watch. Not yet qualified on the operation of the evaporator, it was to my advantage to take this punishment with a little joy. By the time my still watch was over, I had made about fifty gallons of fresh water and knew how to operate the evaporator, which was on my qualification list. Also, I got to know the man on duty in the engine room where the evaporator was located. In addition to making fresh water, I learned the engine room and the main engines.

A few of events during these few months of our operations seem to remain in my memory. First was the time we had a platoon of marines on board. They were in training to launch an undercover assault against an enemy beach. It was very early in the morning, and we had broached the boat to where the deck was just above the surface. I had permission to be on the bridge, so I could watch the operation. The marines were inflating their rubber rafts and getting ready to leave when all of a sudden, a large wave swept over the deck and washed a number of the marines overboard, along with one of the rubber rafts. What a mess! For the next thirty minutes, the marines and the crew assigned to assist were scrambling to get everyone back aboard and ready to go. I found the entire scene rather amusing, as it was like something you would see in a comedy movie. Because of my somewhat loud laughter, the marine lieutenant gave me a rather intimidating look, and the officer of the deck told me to go below.

Another event was when the boat was assigned to go to the island of Maui for R&R. I was surprised the navy would assign a submarine, or any vessel, to a location for R&R (rest and relaxation). I was told it was also to promote public relations with civilians. Although I didn't get to do much sightseeing, I enjoyed being there. We had brought plenty of beer and soda to have barbecues on the beach almost every evening. We also opened the boat for tours to the civilians. Not having much money to go sightseeing, I volunteered to give tours on my days off. One day, after a tour, I was invited by a nice family to have dinner at their home. This was very nice; however, I wasn't a big fan of some of the food I was offered. To this day, I do not eat raw fish or poi!

The entire five days we were in Maui, the entire crew seemed to have a great time. However, should you ask the corpsman, I am sure you would get a different point of view. You see, the corpsman was kept busy patching crew members up. A couple of guys rented a motor scooter and ended up wrecking it and getting severe road rash, while another crew member had too much beer and tried to open a coconut with a bayonet, ending up having to have the bayonet removed from his hand. These and a few other incidents kept the corpsman quite busy.

Having to qualify on the .45-caliber semiautomatic pistol and the .45-caliber Thompson submachine gun was really a fun event. The boat was out in the middle of nowhere in Hawaiian waters. We had surfaced the boat and were on the main deck aft of the sail. Each of us, not qualified, had to load the clips required for each of the weapons and go to the leading torpedoman, the weapons petty officer, one at a time. After the given instructions, we had to shoot at the target, a large box that was thrown into the water, in the prescribed manner taught. Shooting the .45-caliber pistol was fun, but shooting the .45-caliber Thompson was great fun! The torpedoman said we had a large quantity of outdated ammunition that had to be used up. Therefore, any of us that wanted to shoot the Thompson could shoot as much as we wanted, as long as we loaded the clips. I suspect I shot at least a thousand rounds. I was told to shoot in bursts rather continuously. This way, the weapon would not "walk away" from me. The instructor told me I didn't have to kill the enemy (the box), just keep it from being able to get a shot at me. I would have shot more, but we ran out of ammo. Needless to say, I became qualified on both the .45-caliber pistol and the .45-caliber Thompson submachine gun.

The following day, the captain allowed the crew to have swim call. As I said earlier, we were in Hawaiian waters. The water was so clear one could see down seventy-five feet or more. We had two men, from the duty section, with automatic carbine rifles on each side of the bridge as shark watches. The bow planes were lowered to allow easy access to the main deck and for those that didn't want to jump into the water from the main deck. Swim call lasted for over four hours so all duty sections would have an opportunity to swim.

Me standing topside watch on USS *Greenfish SS 351*

After about four and a half months, on the twenty-second of February 1964, I earned the respect and appreciation of the entire crew. We were in port, on standard routine. Skelly, the leading sonarman, sent me after parts for our broken active sonar equipment. I had just returned from retrieving the parts for the active sonar equipment when I heard a loud scream and immediately realized Skelly had suffered a severe electrical shock. I was first on the scene and rendered first aid and took control of the situation, calling out orders to others present—to call for an ambulance, get the corpsman, get some blankets, bring the first aid kit, and provide me with help to get Skelly up to the main deck. Skelly was alive; however, he was very badly hurt. His left hand looked as though it had been put into a deep fat fryer, and the back of his right shoulder looked like he had been shot with a shotgun. My performance was reported to the duty officer by other crew members, and I was given a well-done. I thought that was the end of it. However, about a month later, during a squadron change of command ceremony with five submarines and crews, the base commander, other dignitaries, and guests present, I was awarded a commendation for possibly saving the life of a shipmate and handling a major casualty as a seasoned submariner. From then on, I was considered an asset everywhere I went during my career. When you are transferred, the new command reads the record of newly assigned personnel.

> Note: *As my career continued, I was awarded many other commendations, letters of appreciation, and awards that will be revealed later in the story.*

Prior to going into the Pearl Harbor Shipyard, the boat had to off-load all our torpedoes. Wouldn't you know it? They chose to do this on a Friday! Oh well, that's life! Almost all weapons are off-loaded in West Lock. This is the western lock of Pearl Harbor. You have to understand, the local people in Hawaii speak a mixture of broken English, some Hawaiian, and God only knows what else. We, those of us from the mainland, called it Kanaka. Having only been in Pearl for about four and a half months, I had no idea how to communicate with the locals. Needless to say, most of the civilians working at the weapons depot in West Lock were locals! The crane operators, the line handlers, weapons truck drivers, etc. Well, the boat got moored in West Lock about 10:00; everyone seemed to be at their stations and ready to go. At first, I thought this wasn't going to be so bad after all. We should be able to get all the torpedoes off by 17:00 and go on liberty as planned. Fat chance! Trying to communicate with the locals proved to be a disaster! It took us about one and a half hours to get one torpedo off the boat and onto the weapons truck. At this rate, we would be here until sometime tomorrow. Everyone, locals and crew members, was becoming very upset and angry. Finally, the leading torpedoman came topside. Thank God! He had been stationed in Hawaii over fifteen years and was even married to a local. He could speak Kanaka! He also told the cook to make plenty of hamburgers, enough for the crew and the locals assisting us. Passing out hamburgers sure eased tensions and improved spirits. Believe me, he was a godsend. He communicated to the crew in English and the locals in Kanaka. We started moving torpedoes off the boat in record speed. I think it's safe to say we were able to off-load all the torpedoes by 18:00. Those not in the duty section were able to go on liberty. After that incident, I set out to try and learn Kanaka, or at least understand it.

Shortly after, *Greenfish* went into the naval shipyard at Pearl Harbor for the major overhaul and retrofit. While in the shipyard, I had the opportunity to buy a car. The car was a Ford station wagon with a V-8 engine. It ran extremely poorly, but I felt that with the help of an engineman friend, we could get it running well. A number of my shipmates thought I was out of my mind to buy it. The first thing that my mechanic found was two broken spark plug wires. Replacing them made a tremendous difference. The car now at least ran.

Not having enough money at the time, I partnered with a shipmate to buy the car. It was through this shipmate that I met Derlaann (Derla). It seems one of his shipmates ran into a girl with whom he had gone to high school who was now living on the island. She was from his hometown in Washington State and was living with her sister, who was married to a sailor stationed in Hawaii. My shipmate's buddy asked Laveta (the girl he knew from Washington) to set up a blind date with my car partner. The same night of their date, I also wanted to use the car. Therefore, I agreed to let him use the car, but he had to drop me off at the Queen Surf, a nightclub I liked to frequent, and pick me up after his date.

Apparently, the date did not go very well, as he and his date (Derla) arrived at the Queen Surf before the last show. I told them I wanted to see the last show and invited them to join me. After the show, they sat in the front of the car as I sat in the back while we went to her house. At her house, as my car partner went around the car to open the door for her, she turned to me, gave me her number, and asked me to call her sometime!

Dating Derla

Derla's Senior Picture

While in the Pearl Harbor shipyard, the crew was set up on a barge, near the dry dock where the boat was. It was set up with sleeping quarters and messing facilities. I had done something to upset the COB (chief of the boat), and he assigned me to mess cook. Not having finished my submarine qualification   program, my division officer said his hands were tied until I completed my quals or was promoted to third-class petty officer. However, this, too, had some advantages. First of all, I hate to see food wasted. Therefore, after the entire crew was fed, I asked a few of the shipyard workers if they wanted to eat the leftovers. Within three days, I was feeding about five to six workers every evening. The shipyard workers, in return, had a skiff put outside the galley and told me to put all the garbage into it and they would have the crane operator empty it for me. This saved me about an hour, the time it would take to schlep all the trash up and down several sets of stairs to the dumpster on the pier and back.

USS *Greenfish SS 351* in dry dock

Me being a fool by leaning on dry dock chain

As a mess cook, I did not have to stand duty; hence, I was off every evening and night. Therefore, I was able to work on quals and see Derla every evening she was able to go out. Unfortunately, she was still a senior in high school and could not go out every night. As a matter of fact, she was living with Mr. and Mrs. Hanson as a high school nanny. She was allowed free time after doing her schoolwork and her household chores but had to be in early on school nights. So, although I was off every evening, I didn't get to see Derla each evening. Therefore, I knuckled down to complete my quals program as soon as possible.

Fortunately, I had completed all the at-sea quals prior to entering the shipyard, leaving me with only the remaining items of the fifth, sixth, and seventh month of the seven-month qual program. I completed my qualification in submarines on 18 April 1964, just short of six months. Put another way, I finished my qual program over a month and a half early. Within a couple of days, my division officer had me assigned back into the sonar gang. Now that I was back in the gang, and qualified things were much better, although, on four-section duty, there was little to do in sonar while in overhaul. I was off the entire day after duty, as was the entire duty section, and I was usually off by 14:30 the other off-duty days. Additionally, I was also able to buy out my car partner. He needed money, and I had gotten lucky in a poker game and won a couple hundred dollars. This was more than enough to buy out my car partner.

Speaking of the car, I have to tell you a little about it! I bought the car from a captain's wife who was somewhat naive about automobiles. As I said, the car was running very badly. Hence, I only paid $200 for it. When my mechanic buddy and I looked it over, we noticed a couple of the spark plug wires were broken, causing it to fire on only six of the eight cylinders. Repairing this made a tremendous improvement. However, more work needed to be done. Now that the car was all mine, my buddy and I went to work! We took off the valley cover, the lifter covers, and we drained the oil. Then we used the steam cleaner and steam cleaned everything we could get to. Most of the crew said the car would never run again, but I had confidence in my buddy. After steam cleaning, we put everything back together and filled the crankcase with diesel fuel instead of oil; then turned it over for just about one minute. Then we drained out all the diesel fuel. Boy! All sorts of gunk came out. We did this about three more times until the last drained diesel fuel was free of any gunk. Then we filled the crankcase with oil and ran the engine for about four or five minutes, drained the oil, and inspected it for any clumps or gunk. As the drained oil looked pretty good, we change the oil filter and put in new oil and drove around for about fifteen or twenty minutes. Not only did the car run, it ran and sounded great! Additionally, I had a shipyard welder, I had made friends with, weld in some new floor panels that were almost rusted through and a few other parts that were rusted. (Note: In Hawaii, the salty sea air made cars start rusting in very short order.) With all the repairs we made, I now had an eight-hundred- or nine-hundred-dollar car.

Remember, this was 1964; that was a lot of money! This not only surprised my shipmates, but it also made several envious. It took my buddy and me several days to do all the work on the car. When I got transferred back to the mainland, I sold my car to my friend who helped me get it running so good!

With a good running car and getting off work by 14:00 on my non-duty days, I was provided much more time to see Derla. I would pick her up after school every day I wasn't on duty until she graduated. I even took a few of her friend's home. Derla and I would see each other almost every day and every weekend. Almost every time Derla and I were together, she would dance for me. She would do Hawaiian hulas, Samoan, Tahitian, and Tonganese dances. I had my own private Polynesian shows.

I have to tell you, before leaving Mom and Dad, I told them I was going to Hawaii and going to get a hula girl. *Boy!* That is exactly what I did! You see, during the summer between Derla's junior and senior year, she was part of a Hawaiian dance troop. The troop put on hula shows for the tourists at the International Marketplace in Waikiki.

Derla was *great*! She realized I didn't have much money, only being a seaman, so she would pack a lunch and we would go into the mountains or to the beach on our dates. Derla was very close to her Uncle Billy and Auntie Maka and their children, her cousins. Naturally, we visited them quite often. With them being locals, I was able to begin to understand Kanaka and even learned a few phrases. However, I don't think I will ever like the dried fish, seaweed, and God knows what else they eat. However, the kalua pig, rice, and fresh fruit were really good.

Here, I should slip in another story in regarding the car and Derla. Although the car was in pretty good shape, it did have a problem I felt I would just deal with. It had a broken tooth on the flywheel. This presented a problem when that broken tooth was at the starter pinion positioned when stopped. Although it didn't happen often, it did happen. When it did I had to get the blanket or the cardboard I kept in the car and use it to allow me to get under the car and use a large flat blade screwdriver to shift the flywheel, so the starter would engage. On one such evening I was about to take Derla home from our date when the starter did not engage. So, under the car I went.

To my unpleasant surprise I saw a number of locals coming our way. Why was I concerned? Well! It was not uncommon for locals to beat military members to a pulp when caught with local girls. So I said to myself, "if I'm to be turned into mincemeat, I should try and take as many of them as I could with me!" Fortunately, the locals were Derla cousins coming to see if they could help. Boy, what a relief!

One of our favorite places to go on our dates was Hanauma Bay. This is a very beautiful place. The movie *"Blue Hawaii"* was filmed there. Back in the early to mid-1960s, Hanauma Bay hadn't been discovered by the tourists. There probably weren't more than ten people there at any time we went. We would spend the entire day either lying on the beach or snorkeling. One event, while snorkeling, I will never forget. I went down to about twenty feet to observe the many different kinds of fish and all the beautiful colors. I was so moved by the sight, I smiled. That was not the right thing to do. By smiling, I broke the seal on my mask and let the seawater in. *Damn!* I thought I was going to drown. I couldn't get to the surface fast enough. Let me tell you, no matter how beautiful the ocean may be, it really tastes awful and is not conducive to breathing!

As I said, Derla would pack us a nice lunch or dinner, so we could just be together and enjoy each other. It was great and will always hold fond memories. Today, although still very beautiful, Hanauma Bay is like a tourist trap with literally thousands of people there! To make matters worse, you must pay a fee to go there. Except for the week Derla went to Maui for a family visit, this went on for the entire summer.

Hanauma Bay

It was during her family visit on Maui that I realized I had fallen in love with her. Although she was only gone a week, I missed her terribly. Remember, there were *no* cell phones back then. Writing a letter was futile, as she would be home before her response would reach me. This separation convinced me I wanted to spend the rest of my life with her. Just before Derla went to Maui, I was promoted to submarine sonarman, third class (E-4). I had passed the February 1964 advancement exam and got promoted in May of 1964. Therefore, shortly after she returned from Maui, I asked her to marry me. I felt we would be able to make it now that I was a petty officer. Boy, I had a lot to learn! It was our plan to get married in August and have a short honeymoon in Kauai. This way, we could enjoy a month or so together before *Greenfish* would be deployed to WESTPAC (Western Pacific). Again, the navy had other plans!

While on sea trials, *Greenfish* received a message that the submarine force needed sonarmen for the fleet ballistic missile submarine program (FBM or boomer, as they were called). Hence, I was given orders to advanced sonar training for FBM submarines. At first, I thought I was being punished for something I had done wrong. I tried to reject the orders and pleaded with my division officer and then the executive officer to keep me on board. He insisted I was chosen because of saving the man's life, qualifying in record time, and being promoted to third class in less than two years. He said it would further my career and be in my best interest to accept the orders, as only those who have demonstrated potential were chosen for this assignment. Therefore, I told Derla this would serve as a test to ensure our love for each other. I told her to go out with other guys and I would also go out with other women. After a month or so, if we still felt the same way about each other, we could get married in Atwater, CA., with my family.

Derla insisted the navy was simply trying to prevent our marriage. The submarine force was known to transfer a sailor to help him rid himself of a girl problem back then. Nevertheless, I was transferred to San Diego for advanced sonar training.

Back to San Diego and Marriage

After arriving at the fleet sonar school, I began doing what I had told Derla to do—go out! However, this didn't last very long. It only took a few dates, and I realized the love of my life was in Hawaii. Going out with women, with the hope of having sex, was no longer appealing. I wanted Derla and only Derla! Also, by the fourth week of advanced training, I was again in deep trouble. This training was much harder than initial sonar training. It appeared I was going to be washed out. But there was Chief Keary! At the review board, he went to bat for me. He emphasized my strong points and exaggerated my commendation for saving a life, qualifying in submarines a month and a half early, my promotion to third class in less than two years, and my strong desire to learn. Thanks to Chief Keary, I was given a setback to the next class starting about two weeks later. This provided stress relief and extra time to study.

Feeling confident I was going to get help with this training, I wrote Derla and asked if she still felt the same about me as I did about her. The week to ten days waiting for her reply seemed like an eternity. Remember, this was 1964—no cell phones! After I read her letter, I was filled with joy and happiness. The next day, I purchased a money order for the plane fare from Hawaii to San Francisco, CA, and sent it to her. My shipmates said I would never see that money again. However, I knew better. Derla was to fly to San Francisco where my mother and father would pick her up and take her to their house in Atwater. I would come to Atwater and pick her up and visit with my parents.

While at home, in Atwater, Derla and I went to the Castle Air Force Base Exchange to pick out and buy a wedding ring. Boy, was it small! It was just a small wedding band set with three little diamonds—they looked more like little shards of glass—and an engagement ring set with a slightly larger center diamond and two tiny diamonds, one each side, all in white gold. It wasn't much, but it was all I could afford. The total weight was probably less than one-fourth karat. Derla seemed to be happy with it and never complained. During this first week in California, we planned our wedding. Mom and Dad suggested we get married in their church in Atwater and they would make all the arrangements. To allow time for premarital counseling and getting everything set up, we planned for our marriage to be held on the twenty-second of November 1964. My training at the fleet sonar school would not be in session for Thanksgiving week. Additionally, my training would be completing the first week of December.

As I indicated earlier, Chief Keary was a godsend. He arranged for me to have tutoring at the school and asked a couple of the instructors to give me extra help on their duty days. A few weeks before our marriage, Chief Keary invited Derla and me over to his place for study and barbecue. Chief Keary and I were hitting the books, and Derla and Mrs. Keary were having girl talk. All of a sudden, Chief Keary said, "Enough, you finally get it!" and closed the book. I asked him how he knew; he said I had lit up like a light bulb. It finally all made sense. I understood what was going on. That made the barbecue much more enjoyable. Additionally, the remaining few weeks in school were much more relaxed. Derla and I could enjoy each other with me not constantly worrying if I would make it through school.

As I had sold my car before leaving Hawaii, it was necessary for Derla and me to buy another car. Also, Derla had to learn to drive. Therefore, during the last six weeks of advanced sonar training, we bought a car from a used car lot in San Diego. It was a large 1960 Mercury Monterey. Derla and I practiced driving every day after training for about two weeks. Also, I would quiz Derla with questions from the motor vehicle book we received from the DMV office where she obtained her learner's permit. About a week after our wedding, Derla took and passed her driving test and was able to get around on her own.

As for our wedding, it was during Thanksgiving week, in November 1964. I took a week's leave so Derla and I could go to Atwater, CA.; get married; and visit with my mom and dad. Dad and Mom had made all the arrangements for the wedding. We were to be married in Mom and Dad's church, the First Methodist of Atwater, CA. We had a small rehearsal on Saturday, the twenty-first, and the actual wedding on the afternoon of Sunday, November 22. Our wedding party was very small. For the best man and maid of honor, we used my school friends. Kenny Martin served as best man, and Alice Regan was the maid of honor. My sisters (Roberta and Darlene), my brother (Robert), Aunt Margi and Uncle Stan, and Fay and Travis Marin were the guests present. After the wedding, Dad had arranged for us to have a small reception at the Castle Air Force Base NCO club, with a small wedding cake and some light refreshments with finger food. It really wasn't much of a wedding to remember. None of Derla's family was present, and except for me, Derla felt like a stranger. To this day, neither Derla nor I have very fond memories. As hard as we try, we find it very difficult to remember any of the details, outside a few bits and pieces. I do remember being very scared and, at the same time, very happy. I can only hope and pray Derla, too, was very happy.

Our wedding picture

Before advanced sonar training was complete, all the students were asked to fill out their dream sheets (request for orders). As Derla had never left the Hawaiian Islands, we decided to request Charleston, South Carolina, as my home port. This would give Derla a chance to see how big the United States really is, from coast to coast. Not wanting to live in an area with a lot of snow, I did not request the submarine base at New London, Connecticut, or Norfolk, Virginia. To our surprise, I received orders to Charleston, South Carolina. However, to my dismay, my orders were to the USS *Trout* SS 566. This was *not* a fleet ballistic missile submarine. It was a diesel fast attack. It sure makes you wonder how the navy works.

Off to Charleston, South Carolina

We packed up the car with all our belongings (we really didn't have anything but the clothes on our back) and headed to Charleston. Trying to save money, we decided to sleep in the car and drive straight through. We were young and didn't know any better. The trip took about four days. This was 1964, and there were no interstates then. We would buy most of our food at grocery stores and stop at roadside rest spots to make our lunch and dinner. Seldom would we eat at a restaurant. Saving money was paramount, as we would need to get an apartment when we arrived in Charleston.

One event during the trip seems to stick out in my mind. I had been sleeping in the back seat when I felt the car stop. Upon opening my eyes, I noticed we were at a gas station. Looking at the gas pump, I noticed the price per gallon was only *eleven cents* a gallon. I could not believe my eyes. I called out to the attendant and said there was something wrong with his pump. He assured me all was okay and said the reason for the low price was a gas war between local gas stations. *We will never see that again!*

The afternoon we arrived in Charleston, we checked into a hotel for a couple of days. It was great to sleep in a real bed and take a bath or a shower. Also, this allowed me time to go to the boat, report in, meet some shipmates, and try to get some ideas where we could get an apartment. It was suggested we go to Folly Beach. It was winter, and the apartments would be very cheap. So Folly Beach it was. The apartment we had was just a little one-bedroom, one-bath—actually a shower—with a living room and a very small kitchen. It did serve the purpose; however, it was a long way from the naval base and naval hospital. Why would I be concerned about the naval hospital, you ask. Well, Derla was pregnant!

It was during this time that Derla and I were in the most destitute financial position of our lives. I was only a third-class petty officer (E-4) and barely made enough money to pay the rent and buy food. We were lucky if we had two nickels to rub together between paydays. We had to go without many things, so we could save to buy what was necessary for the baby we were about to have. Let me tell you, I couldn't have picked a better wife. Derla never complained and even washed our clothes in the sink and hung them throughout the apartment to dry. When we bought food, Derla would only buy that which we had to have! She would make meals that we could eat one day and have as leftovers the next day. These meals were very cheap. Derla could spice up hot dogs and beans to give a very tasty flavor and put it over rice. Also, she would make corn beef and cabbage to be put over rice, although that was not as tasty! She is the most frugal woman I have ever seen. God truly blessed me when he brought us together!

USS *Trout SS 566*

My tour on the *Trout* turned out to be very short—less than nine weeks. I remember only going to sea once, and that was for only about a week. This was fine with me. I could be home with Derla every evening I didn't have duty. It was a bit puzzling, however, to come in one morning and be told to gather up all my gear and take it with me to the USS *Sennet* SS 408. I thought I had done something wrong and was being canned. I was assured I was not. The *Sennet* had lost all but one of her sonarmen to FBM Sonar Maintenance School. Still, this did not make much sense to me. After all, I was FMB sonar trained and hence should be on an FBM? *Go figure!*

Off to the *Sennet* I went. It wasn't a very long trip. The *Sennet* was moored on the same pier. It took all of five minutes to walk to her and check in. From the beginning, I had the feeling I was not going to like this assignment. Although most of the crew were friendly and welcomed me aboard, the leading chief was a converted electronics technician (ET) and, in my opinion, left a lot to be desired.

The *Sennet* was a World War II submarine and actually had made four World War II patrols. Although the *Sennet* had an impressive war record, she had very little postwar modifications and was not to my liking. The only redeeming value to being assigned to the *Sennet* was that she was a submarine! The *Sennet* would be my assignment for a little over four months. During that time, I spent about two and a half months at sea, leaving Derla alone like many other navy wives.

USS *Sennet SS408* entering Curacao Harbor

While on the *Sennet,* we went to the islands of Cuba, Saint Thomas, and Curacao. This deployment lasted about a month. As Curacao was one of the Netherland Antilles, we were the guest of the Dutch Navy. We spent about four days in port and were given tours of the island and were given island liberty. After the four days of R&R (rest and relaxation), we operated with the Dutch Navy, playing hide-and-seek. The Dutch Navy had about ten or twelve observers on board.

It should be noted that the *Sennet* had a crack in number 3 fuel ballast tank. This proved to be a problem; as we were leaking fuel oil everywhere we went. *So!* We left an oil slick!

Leaving an oil slick made hiding from the Dutch Navy next to impossible! Therefore, it was decided to pump all the remaining fuel oil in number 3 fuel ballast to another tank and blow the tank dry. This procedure was not thought out very well! You see, blowing a tank that has a crack in will not hold air very well. Hence, when we blew all tanks to surface, we surfaced with a large list to starboard (right). Additionally, all the air rushing through the crack made a very loud howling sound. This literally scared the bejesus out of our Dutch observers. Can you imagine never having been on a submarine and suddenly coming up with a large starboard list making it very difficult to stand up and hearing a loud howling sound? To add insult to injury, we surfaced in our own oil slick. *Boy! What a mess.* You see, when the hatch is opened after being submerged, it is not uncommon for about one to two gallons of water to come into the boat. Only this time, it wasn't water; it was fuel oil and water mixed—all over the ladder, conning tower deck, and even down into the control room. Smelly, slippery, and foamy, it took several weeks to really clean it all up!

On our way home, we received a message to return to Charleston as soon as possible, replenish fuel and supplies, and make way to rendezvous with a HUK force (Hunter/ Killer force made of ships and submarines) off Cape Hatteras, North Carolina. I did not even get a chance to go home to see Derla. I had duty and had to stay on board. This really upset me, and I decided to do all I could to get transferred to a boomer (fleet ballistic missile submarine) as fast as possible.

The next morning, we set out to meet up with the HUK force. This turned out to be about eight days of misery. After all, it was over a month since I had been with Derla, and the weather was absolutely atrocious. Most of the time, we could not submerge because of the very bad weather. (Note: World War II submarines had to ride storms out on the surface. This is because if, for any reason, the boat had to surface, a strong wave hitting the boat just right could flip the boat over while surfacing.) Almost the entire crew was seasick. Let me tell you, the boat smelled very badly from crew members upchucking. Even if the rough seas didn't make you sick, the terrible smell sure did!

We kept receiving orders to transit to a new operation area to try to find an area that was not stormy. On one such transit, I was operating the radar. The weather was so bad we had strapped in the lookouts and duty officer on the bridge. Also, we closed the conning tower hatch to keep the seawater from coming in. It was during this time I decided to show my displeasure by taunting the duty officer. Every time I saw a big wave on the radar, I would call up to the bridge and say something like "Hang on to your hat, another *big* wave is coming" or "Here comes another one."

This went on for about half an hour before the duty officer had had enough! He ordered the radar operator (me) to the bridge. So, to the bridge I went. When I reached the bridge, I asked what he wanted, and he said to stay for a short visit. Just then, I saw a huge wave coming toward the bridge. Forgetting the entire bridge area was a free-flood area, I jumped onto the chart table in the dog house, an area under cover used for charting and such. Although I did not get wet from the wave that engulfed the bridge, I soon found myself swimming in the dog house as the water from the wave flooded through the entire free-flood area. Now that I was completely soaked, I told the duty officer he had made his point and asked if I could go below and resume my duties on the radar. When I got off watch, I went to my locker and changed into dry clothes and kept my mouth shut.

About a week later, in early May of 1965, we were back in port and on shore routine. During some free time, I walked over to squadron personnel and made my case to be transferred to a missile boat. Squadron assured me they knew I was on the *Sennet* and would be transferred to the USS *James Madison SSBN 627 (Gold)* as soon as she came off patrol. The USS *James Madison SSBN 627 (Gold)* crew arrived in port about a week later, and I received my transfer orders. This was much better! I reported on board during the beginning of the R&R period. The crew had to report on Monday, Wednesday, and Friday morning at 08:00 for muster and was released about an hour later, unless you had duty. Additionally, duty was only once every twenty-five days.

USS *James Madison SSBN 627*

This was another godsend assignment! Derla was about eight and a half months pregnant at this time, and I was able to be with her. We spent almost every day walking up and down the beach, awaiting the arrival of our firstborn. During this time, my dad, mom, sisters, and brother stopped by for a very quick visit. My dad was still in the US Air Force and had orders to Germany. Therefore, they decided to say hi on their way to Dover Air Force Base for a flight to Germany. Although it was a very short visit, it was great to see them.

On the night of June 27, 1965, Derla said it was time to go to the hospital. It was over twenty miles from Folly Beach to the naval hospital. I was speeding as fast as the road conditions would allow, hoping a police car would see me so I could have an escort. Wouldn't you know it! Never is there a policeman around when you want one!

Back in 1965, husbands and family members were not allowed to be in the labor room with expectant mothers, so I waited in the waiting room all night. Our first son, Freddy (Fred Bryce Maphis), was born about 08:30 in the morning on the twenty-eighth of June 1965. To this day, I remember driving back to Folly Beach with my head so big it was hard to get into the car.

We spent the next twelve to thirteen months in Charleston. However, we moved from Folly Beach into an apartment in town (Charleston) near the base. The main reason for moving was due to the landlord and how prejudiced he and his wife were. I had invited a young black boy into my apartment to take a break and have some water. It was a very hot summer day. He was clearing tall weeds in the open field next to the apartment. Remember, they didn't have weed eaters back then; therefore, it was very strenuous work using a sickle. I had just arrived home, and he asked if he could have a drink of water from my garden hose. I told him that water would taste foul and to come in, have water from my tap, and rest a minute or two. The next day, the landlord said we do not allow blacks into our homes for such reasons. I was really taken aback at this attitude, especially because he had invited Derla and me to attend their church. I asked him what kind of Bible he and his church used! My Bible said nothing about blacks or any other colored person not being allowed in a white person's home. I called him a hypocrite and moved out within a week.

While on the *Madison*, I made two FBM patrols and was promoted to STS2 (SS). Making an FBM patrol requires being away from home, like any other type of military deployment. However, a missile submarine deployment requires family members to be completely isolated. There is absolutely no communication back home. Once the submarine is deployed, *no one* knows anything until the deployment is complete and the submarine surfaces.

In 1965, the *James Madison* was operating out of Rota, Spain. Therefore, the crew had to fly to Rota and relieve the alternating crew.

> Note: *In order for a fleet ballistic missile submarine to be an effective deterrent, it had to be on deployment constantly. Subsequently, each deterrent missile submarine has two crews, blue and gold. In this way, the submarine was only in port long enough to change crews, refit, and replenish supplies, keeping you away from home between ninety to one hundred days.*

Once on the boat, I was assigned my berth and locker. Not knowing how clean the previous person using this locker and berth was, I decided to really clean it. I went to the base exchange and bought a spray can of Lysol. I spent almost two hours using soap and water, scrubbing the entire berth, mattress cover, and locker. After I felt it was nice and clean, I sprayed the berth, mattress cover, locker, and even the mattress with the entire can of Lysol to kill any remaining possible germs. This smelled up the entire berthing area. Numerous crew members asked me *what the hell I was doing*. I told them I didn't know what kind of person had this berth before me and I wanted to be sure it was clean and I was *not* going to catch anything. From then on, my nickname on the *Madison* was Lysol. (Note: I pretty much did this to all my berthing assignments!)

Knowing I was going to be at sea for about sixty days or more and unable to communicate with Derla, I had an idea that might help Derla cope with such a long period of *no* communication and of separation.

> Note: *The crew was allowed to receive only three fifteen-word telegrams if message traffic would allow. Remember, this was the '60s, and communication was not as advanced as today.*

My idea was to befriend a crew member of the sonar shop on the submarine tender to mail a large number of prewritten letters for Derla. So I decided to write about thirty to thirty-five letters and put the date I wanted the letters mailed where the stamp was to be placed. In this way, Derla would receive a letter about every other day, depending on the postal service. This was a little harder than it sounds. Have you ever tried to write something you might say three weeks from now? Some of the letters didn't say much of anything other than "I love you." Nevertheless, Derla would get a letter at least several times a week and have something to look forward to. Sometimes I would try and guess how many days of separation were left and say "Only about fourteen more days until I will be home" or "Only another week!" This proved to be a big surprise to Derla, so I continued doing it every time I was deployed.

During my first FBM patrol, I was determined be promoted! To ensure I would pass the STS 2 (SS) test, I read every book on sonar I had access to that was in the sonar area, in addition to the course books. This was a wise idea. The promotion exam was during our time in port and seemed rather easy to me; all that reading and studying paid off. I also wanted to prove my worth as a valuable asset to the crew, so I endeavored to re-qualify on the *Madison*.

Note: *Every submariner must re-qualify when transferred to another submarine, in order to "know the boat."*

During my second patrol, the results of the promotion exam were received, and I was promoted to submarine sonarman second class STS 2 (SS). Additionally, we were all in for a surprise. As it turned out, the *Madison* was going to test a number of missiles. Naturally, they were not armed; they were checking accuracy. In a way, this made the patrol go by much faster for me. Although I did my prewritten letters again, I was able to call home when we completed our missile shoot and came back into port to replenish the fired practice missiles with armed missiles.

The missile shoot was a little troublesome. The entire world was told a submarine was going to have a practice missile shoot. This was so no country would fear being attacked. Needless to say, Russian trawlers, various surface warships, and even submarines were all over the place trying to watch and see how well our missile weapons system worked. We had to be on constant alert to avoid a possible collision and listen for other submarines. This went on for the entire time we fired our five practice missiles. After the shoot, we went deep, ensured we were not picked up by any Russians, and headed back to Rota.

Me topside on "Madison" while in the
harbor in Rota, Spain

After replacing the fired practice missiles, we went back out on patrol into the North Atlantic. During this patrol, we encountered an unpleasant surprise. We heard sonar pinging and were scrambling to ascertain the type of sonar and type of vessel, all the while trying to remain undetected. The captain, executive officer (XO), and division officer were constantly telling us to recheck our findings! We had told them that it was 23 sonar on a US destroyer leader. The captain wasn't buying it! He insisted we were in error and said it had to be Russian! After checking and double-checking, we told the captain that we either needed to be given more information that we felt he was holding back or it indeed was a US destroyer leader with 23 sonar. As the cat-and-mouse game continued, I believed the surface craft may have actually picked us up! As a result, the captain gave orders to *go deep* and evade. Within a few minutes, we were no longer in harm's way and were out of the area. About a day later, our division officer came in and gave us a "well done!" We had received a message that a US warship was going to be in our patrol area and that we had to be on the alert. It made the entire sonar gang look good for saying and sticking to our assessment.

As we were operating in the North Atlantic Ocean, we had the occasion to cross the Arctic Circle. This was a momentous occasion! Crossing the Arctic Circle is somewhat analogous to crossing the equator. All those that had never crossed the Arctic Circle, or the equator, must undergo an initiation to become a blue nose for the Arctic Circle or a shell back for crossing the equator. The initiation process is not the most pleasant ordeal, but it was all in fun. For the most part, all the initiates were accommodating. You see, you have to kiss "King Neptune's" belly and pick a cherry out of his navel. They would use the fattest sailor on board and smear his belly with all sorts of yucky stuff—stuff like sardines, cayenne pepper, and anything that would taste horrible. Also, a haircut was called for. Unfortunately, the haircut was as ugly and grotesque as possible. Additionally, a bluing compound was put on our noses. Boy, it took about four days to get that stuff off my nose. There were a few other things we had to endure, but it was all tolerable. After the initiation, we were all members of the royal order of blue nose. There is even an entry noted in each person's personnel record.

As I was nearing the end of my first enlistment and being a good sailor, I was approached several times to reenlist. Having been a good shipmate; promoted to E-5 in less than four years; a recipient of a commendation, Good Conduct Medal, and National Defense Medal; and an asset to the crew, I was able to negotiate a tour of shore duty back in Hawaii in return for reenlisting. At this time, the navy was awarding large bonuses to those in critical rates for reenlisting. This provided Derla and me with a very nice chunk of change, which surely improved our financial posture.

Back to Pearl Harbor, Hawaii

Being second class was great! I was now considered a seasoned submariner and no longer a low man on the totem pole. Also, as an E-5, the navy would not only transfer me, it would also transfer my family, my car, and my belongings. This would be done at the navy's expense.

> Note: *An enlisted man had to either have four years of service or be an E-5 before the government would pay all travel expenses for the family upon being transferred.*

Before leaving Charleston, we bought a new car and took a month of travel time and leave to drive to California where we were to pick up our flight to Hawaii and ship our car. During the month-long drive, we did a little sightseeing. We visited Carlsbad Caverns; Derla's uncle in Walla Walla, Washington; and my relatives and friends in Atwater, California.

We arrived in Hawaii in August of 1966. I reported for duty at the submarine base of Pearl Harbor (SUBASE PEARL). We were provided TLA (temporary lodging allowance) while we waited to be assigned base housing. I was assigned to SUBASE shop 67G. Shop 67 was the electronics repair shop on the repair base, and the G section was for sonar.

The sonar section was not very large. We had about four people—a first-class, me, and two seamen. The entire shop (which was divided into numerous sections) had about forty to fifty members, most of whom were second- and third-class petty officers. I felt this was going to be a good assignment. The shop was on six-section duty. This allowed me to be home five nights in every six. I thought it was great!

After about two weeks, we were assigned to temporary base housing (NHA 3), awaiting permanent base house. These quarters were old units that were in the process of being replaced. Nevertheless, they were okay. In about six months, we were assigned to a two-bedroom unit in Moanalua Terrace, right next to a golf course.

The first-class in charge of the sonar section was awaiting transfer and pretty much let me run the section. This made the assignment even better. Both the leading chief, Chief Wagner, and officer in charge (OIC), Lieutenant Berg, were great to work for. Here again, I was in the right place at the right time.

Within six months, the sonar section was assigned a special task to install a visibility system on the USS *Blackfin* (SS 322). This project was from the secretary of the navy and had a representative from Scripps Institute of Technology, Mr. Tate, as the lead engineer.

USS *Blackfin SS 322*

It appears Mr. Tate was not very trusting of navy-enlisted men. It seems this project was done in San Diego, California, and it went very badly. It took all the diplomacy I could muster to convince Mr. Tate that not all sailors were incapable of doing a good job! So for about the next three weeks, I was extremely busy working with a specific shipfitter, designing and fabricating the necessary sensor mountings, running cables, making pressure hull penetrations, and building the electronic consul. After everything was complete, all that remained was obtaining power from the submarine's electrician. This proved to be a daunting task, as the ship's company was either very busy or not interested in helping! Therefore, I urged Mr. Tate to use his clout to convince the operations officer to allow me to run the necessary power cable to an available power panel and connect it. I informed the operations officer I had qualified on the USS *Greenfish*, which was the same class of submarine as the *Blackfin*, and I knew what I was doing.

I showed the *Blackfin*'s operations officer that I had located a fuse panel with spare hookup terminals and had even run the power cable to that location. He agreed, and I made the electrical connections. Mr. Tate and I began exercising the system through all its preliminary tests. All that was left was to test the system at sea. Mr. Tate requested I ride the USS *Blackfin* to sea for the final checkout and testing. We were at sea for about four days, running the system through all its functions at various depths. The entire system worked flawlessly! Mr. Tate was ecstatic!

Shortly after, about a month or so, during a command presentation, I was ordered to be present and in dress uniform. To my pleasant surprise, I was awarded a commendation for my outstanding work performance and leadership ability. The remainder of my tour at SUBASE PEARL was indeed very good!

During my three years at SUBASE PEARL, I earned the respect and reputation as being one of the best SUBSAFE hull-penetration experts on base. Additionally, I was tasked with all special projects and installations and with outfitting boats that were to be deployed on northern runs with special stuff.

As you may guess, northern runs were to go spy on the Russians. I can say without hesitation that my three-year tour at SUBASE PEARL was very enjoyable. I would have stayed there forever if the navy would have let me.

There are too many stories I could tell of the various jobs and tasks I was assigned. Therefore, I will only relate a few. Early on, I learned not to trust anyone when it pertained to work I had to do. After only a few months, the sonar section was asked to repair a sheared snorkel electrode cable. The snorkel electrodes are used to detect water at the snorkel valve and to close the valve to prevent water from coming into the snorkel mast should a big wave come along. A striker (a new person learning) and I went to the submarine in question with all our equipment and requested that the entire snorkel system be tagged and locked out. After a short while, we were assured by the below-decks watch that the system was safe to work on. To my chagrin, power was still applied to the cables, and I received a severe electrical shock. Were it not for my striker, I could have easily drowned. The shock caused me to hit my head against the side of the submarine's sail and knocked me out. My striker held me and prevented me from sliding into the water. From then on, I either did the tag and lock-out myself or witnessed it being done!

One afternoon, just before the end of the day, a young lieutenant came into the shop looking for me. He was from the USS *Sea Dragon SSN 584.* As it turned out, the *Sea Dragon* had a leaking hull fitting in their after-escape trunk. Unfortunately, the ship had no more funds to repair the leak and was scheduled to go to sea in a couple of days. The lieutenant said he heard I was the best man to repair the hull fitting and would do the work for "*love of God* and *country*" and a case of steaks. I informed him I was not authorized to do such things. You must be careful; someone may be trying to trap you. He then said the steaks would be for the shop to have during a beer ball game after PT (physical training). When I realized he was not trying to get me trapped, I asked my striker if he wanted some steak to take home for about two to three hours of work. After he said yes, we gathered up our tools and went down to the *Sea Dragon*. The hull fitting was truly a mess! It was behind the ladder and full of rust. I had the ship's company take down the ladder and provide me with soap and water to clean away as much rust as I could. Then we worked to free the locking bolt so we could take the fitting apart completely. We ended up using the strongest man in the duty section on the boat to assist us. After using oil of wintergreen, WD-40, and his strength, we got the locking bolt off. After about two additional hours, we completely rebuilt the hull fitting and put it all back together. We never heard from the *Sea Dragon* again regarding this leak, so I can only surmise it was a job well done. All the while, my striker and I enjoyed sharing a small case of steaks.

While the USS *Pickerel SS 524* was in the dry dock, I was assigned the task of making a hull penetration for the installation of some special equipment. This was a routine assignment that I was well acquainted with. However, it did require entering the ballast tank to reach the required location. While in the ballast tank, I noticed a badly corroded pipe not far from my location. I told my striker to note the exact location, so we could bring it to the attention of the topside watch, knowing that if the corroded pipe was not replaced or repaired, it would cause problems when the boat left the dry dock. Therefore, when my striker and I completed our task, we told the topside watch to be sure and have the ship's company address the problem before the boat left the dry dock. Additionally, I insisted he enter it in the log. It was to my good fortune I insisted it be entered in the log, as a few days later, I was called down to the boat, being accused of fouling the hull penetration as the boat was listing and leaking air. When I arrived at the pier, a young lieutenant began shouting that I was the one that created the problem. I simply told the young lieutenant, in front of the skipper, squadron engineer, and a few other high-ranking officers, that I would be sure I knew what I was talking about before making accusations. While we were waiting for both the SUBASE and boat divers to come up, I went to the topside log and located the page I had the topside watch make the entry while they were in dry dock. Sure enough, when the divers got to the surface, they said the problem was a break in the piping that was corroded. I pointed out to all where I had it put in the log and said that it needed to be addressed. Needless to say, that young lieutenant had egg all over his face, and I came out smelling like a rose.

The submarine's name escapes me at this writing; however, this assignment turned out to be a rather compelling job. The normal time needed to outfit a submarine with the necessary equipment to make a northern run is about three weeks. In this case, I only had about fifteen days. The ship fitters and I were working about sixteen to eighteen hours a day in order to get all the hull mountings completed. Then I had to make all the required hull penetrations, mount junction boxes, and perform the internal wiring. This truly took a toll on me. One of my men was on leave, causing me and one other to work over seventeen hours a day. As I was in the final stages of completing the installation, I was in a very tight location in the submarine, making internal wiring connections. It was about 10:00 Saturday morning, after working eighteen hours Thursday and all-day Friday and Friday night to the present, when the below-decks watch found me and asked if I was Maphis. I told him yes, and he said I had a phone call in control. This was somewhat annoying, as it took almost five minutes to get into the tight location where the junction box I was wiring was located. When I got to control and answered the phone, it was the squadron engineer wanting to know how things were going, as the submarine was to leave on patrol Monday morning. I literally lost it! They had me doing a job shorthanded, in ten days less than the average installation. I hollered at him, stating I had been working over eighteen hours a day for the last twelve days and had currently been up for over twenty-four hours trying to get the job completed. Then I chastised him for knowing how much time was required for this type of installation and only affording me half that time with a man short. I continued with how I was exhausted and was going home to bed, then hung up. I then realized what I had just done and figured my career was over. I said to myself, "Well, I am already in trouble, I might as well go home to bed." As I was leaving the boat, the squadron engineer met me on the pier. I figured my goose was cooked! To my surprise, he told me to get some needed sleep and come back Sunday morning. Boy, it was a good thing I had a good reputation! On Sunday morning, I continued where I left off and began checking everything for proper working condition. By then, it was about 09:30 Monday morning, and the boat was supposed to be underway at 08:00. To my surprise, no one bothered me. This allowed me to complete all my checks and leave the boat at about 10:00. The squadron engineer, the boat skipper, and the officer of the deck were at the bow and asked me if everything was ready for sea. I told them everything should work as required and to have a good hunt.

Another story that comes to mind was during the installation of special equipment for another submarine going on a northern run for special operations. The captain of the boat I was working on apparently was observing me and requested I accompany them on the trip. I informed the captain that I appreciated the offer but knew what they were going to do and where they were going to do it. I informed him I would rather stay in Pearl. He stated my expertise would be invaluable and an asset to the operation. I informed him that the special detachment that would be assigned were more qualified than me and would never allow me to operate the equipment. Nevertheless, it was a welcome compliment and added favor to my status. However, in retrospect, I feel I should have accepted the invitation and gone on the run. I would have gained valuable experience and possibly another commendation.

While in Pearl, Derla and I worked hard to get ahead. She and I worked part-time at Mid Pacific Country Club during parties, weddings, and special occasions. I also worked as a waiter, busboy, bar back, bartender, or whatever was needed, while Derla worked as a waitress. Sometimes we would work as a team for small parties. Additionally, I had a part-time job working as the lead bartender at the Beaman Center White Hat Bar on the submarine base.

Speaking of Beaman Center, I recall another incident that took place while I was tending bar. Beaman Center is a large ballroom with many tables and chairs, a stage, and a dance floor. On the right and left side near the back are the White Hat Bar (E1–E4) and the Acey Ducey Bar (E5–E6). It was a typical Friday evening, with a band playing, people dancing, and others in either of the bars enjoying themselves. In the White Bar, where I was working, there was an individual that surely had had too much to drink. He was becoming rather obnoxious and crude with the waitresses. I told him to settle down and control himself. He then became rather abusive toward me. This was his mistake! Being young and dumb and believing myself to be invincible, I grabbed a bottle of liquor from the bar well (the container holding the bar whiskey, vodka, scotch, bourbon, and sour mix), put my foot on the beer cooler and flew over the bar, grabbed the drunk sailor by his shirt collar, and threatened to bust the bottle over his head if he didn't leave immediately. I then proceeded to take him to the exit. (Note: This sailor was about an inch or two taller and probably had fifty pounds on me.) By the next morning, that incident was talked about all over the base. Many of my shipmates told me to remind them not to piss me off!

Derla and I did this part-time work the entire time we were in Pearl. It was our goal to acquire all the things we needed to fill our home and provide for ourselves, our children, with what we needed. Additionally, we wanted to save money. Never again did we want to be in the destitute financial position we were in while in Folly Beach!

After my three-year tour at SUBASE PEARL, I was due to receive orders to go back to sea. Being concerned about what type of orders I might receive, I decided to call on a friend I had made while in the SUBASE bowling league. My friend was a PM (personnel man) assigned to SUBPAC (Submarine Force Pacific). He had me contact one of his friends stationed at the assignment desk in San Diego. By doing this, I was able to get orders to the USS *Benjamin Franklin Blue SSBN 640.*

Contacting my friend also proved to be another godsend. To my surprise, I already had orders to sea on the USS *Snook SSN 592.* The orders were in route and were expected to arrive in a few days. The USS *Snook* was a fast attack submarine. Almost all fast attack submarines have long deployments; they seem to go to sea and get lost! This would have kept Derla and me apart for most of the time I had left on active duty. It would have been a disaster, as Derla was pregnant with our second child and was due in less than two months. I was fortunate enough to convince the person at the assignment desk that I was not qualified to serve on the *Snook* because I was not trained on the type of sonar used on that class of submarine. I was trained to work on and operate the type of sonar used on missile submarines.

By using a little trickery, I had obtained information that would allow me to remain in port for most of the time I had left on active duty. I had the names of three missile (boats) submarines that would afford me the benefit of only having enough time to make one deterrent patrol deployment. I figured that with three boat options, there was sure to be an opening on one of the boats. The person at the assignment desk must have been in good spirits, as he was able to cancel the orders to the *Snook* and assign me to my first choice, the USS *Benjamin Franklin Blue* (SSBN 640). Assignment to the *Franklin* not only afforded me the benefit of making one patrol during my last year of active duty, but it also allowed me to be home for the birth of our second child and for both Thanksgiving and Christmas. Daddy always told me to learn the system and make the system work for you.

USS *Benjamin Franklin SSBN 640*

My last year on active duty worked out to be pretty good after all. Even though I had to go back to sea, having orders to the USS *Benjamin Franklin Blue* worked out great. You see, the *Blue* crew was still on patrol. Therefore, I had to report to the squadron and be assigned to temporary duty to wait for the blue crew to get back into port. My temporary duty assignment was to the squadron duty driver group. The duty drivers were to provide transportation to anyone or to the dependent of anyone in the squadron who needed transportation. Boy, what a cushy job! The duty drivers were on six-section duty and only had to work about seven hours a day. Not only was this assignment great, but the other duty drivers were guys just like me, men waiting for further assignment to their respective boats. We all got along great and would help each other out if we needed to take a little time off. I worked as a squadron duty driver from about

April of 1969 until the blue crew of the USS *Benjamin Franklin* arrived in port, which was about June of 1969.

As I said, Derla was pregnant with our second child. She went into labor on May 24, 1969. This was a surprise, as she was not due until mid-June. Fortunately, I was able to get a few days off and be with Derla. The doctor believed Derla needed a C-section to prevent any mishaps. Robby (Robert Bryon Maphis), our second son, was born the afternoon of 24 May 1969. Robby was about four or five weeks early and had to be in an incubator for about two weeks, until his lungs were more developed and could grow a little stronger. By the time he was ready to come home, Derla had recovered pretty well from the C-section. Then in June, I was transferred to the *Benjamin Franklin Blue*.

The *Benjamin Franklin Blue* turned out to be a great assignment. I reported aboard a day or two after the crew arrived in port. Let me repeat, the crew was in port, not the submarine. The submarine was deployed with the gold crew. As was the custom, the first twenty to thirty days after a deployment, the entire crew was given R&R (rest and relaxation). This was great; we only had to appear in person on Wednesday of each week and call in on Monday and Friday. So I was able to be home with Derla, Freddy, and Robby almost the entire month of June. I was only on duty once, as we only had duty every twenty days or so.

The next two months were filled with training and refresher courses, which took place during the day. The training and refresher courses were to ensure the entire crew was trained and brought current on the latest and greatest associated with their job and duty assignments.

It didn't take me long to fit in as a crew member. As I mentioned earlier, the captain, my division officer, and a few other necessary personnel had access to my personnel file, making them aware of my exploits and achievements. Additionally, the crew was very easy to get to know and become a part of. I was informed I was going to be assigned sonar supervisor for one of the three sections when on deployment. It seems I was the third senior man in sonar and had prior experience on deployments at sea. This was very pleasing to me, as it recognized my skills and leadership ability.

About a month before we deployed, Mr. Holmberg, the executive officer, and my division officer called me into their offices every few days to try and get me to reenlist for a third time. I kept telling them I really liked my job and was happy with the navy; however, I did not like being separated from my family. Therefore, I had decided to leave the navy when my time was up. After several visits, Mr. Holmberg realized I was not going to change my mind. He asked me how I knew the ship's schedule. I said that I did not know anything. He then smiled and told me to see the ship's yeoman and tell him when I wanted out after the deployment. He was authorized to allow me to get out up to 180 days early. So, I told the yeoman to set my release from active duty any time after my entitled R&R. This would set my release from active duty in January of 1970.

The reason I could be released early was simple. The *Benjamin Franklin* was slated to traverse the Panama Canal during what would have been my second patrol (deployment). I would not have had enough time left on my enlistment contract to complete the operation. Remember when I stated I wanted the *Benjamin Franklin* as my first choice? I had found out a little more than I should have. Good old Dad. "Learn the system, then make the system work for you." I knew the next deployment was going to be an extended patrol to traverse the Panama Canal to go to the shipyard for an overhaul. The extra time this would take would put me past my discharge date. Hence, I would not make the next deployment and would be too short to go anywhere else. Therefore, I preferred to have an early out. Finally, by the end of August, the dreaded time to deploy had arrived. Although I was excited to get underway and prove my ability, I detested leaving Derla and my sons. Such is the life of a sailor! We were flown from Pearl Harbor to Agana, Guam. There, about twenty of us (the senior members of the crew and the officers) were taken to a fleet tug (a tugboat able to traverse the ocean), and we met the *Franklin* out at sea. Our job was to spend a day or two with the gold crew going over all the ship's systems and equipment and note all things that were in need of repair or replacement prior to the *Franklin* coming into port.

A day or two later, our crew relieved the gold crew, and we spent about three weeks getting the ship ready to deploy. During this time, I was kept busy performing my responsibilities, working with the entire sonar gang, insuring all our systems were up and running at 100 percent. I remember one evening, during the evening meal, complaining to some of the more senior crew members about the food every time a certain cook was on duty. I was told not to worry. He really was not the cook. He was the baker when on patrol.

The time to deploy had arrived, and all my prewritten letters were given to a reliable individual in the sonar shop on the submarine tender (a large repair ship designed to support submarines). For the next sixty or so days, we were under the ocean in stealth mode. As before, we were in three-section duty, with each section being six hours, making for an eighteen-hour day. Although there are twenty-four hours in the day (00:00–06:00, 06:00–12:00, 12:00–18:00, 18:00–24:00), your watch started every eighteen hours. Hence, you were on watch six hours and off twelve hours. Therefore, every three days, I would be on the midwatch (00:00–06:00). I really looked forward to the midwatch. The *baker* could *really bake*! The entire submarine would smell wonderful once the aroma of fresh bread, cake, pastries, or whatever he was baking entered the ventilation system. About 03:30, during the midwatch, I would go down to the galley and pick up fresh donuts or some other type of sticky buns and coffee and bring them back to the sonar shack (room). My section would enjoy the remainder of the watch, and we really didn't need to go to breakfast when we were relieved by the next watch. Boy, it is a wonder I didn't get *fat*.

This patrol went by rather smoothly for me. I had informed my division officer that I was not going to requalify the boat. As the re-qual program allowed two patrols and because I was only going to make one, I saw no need. Therefore, my division officer worked out a plan requiring me to re-qual on everything from the bow to the end of the missile compartment. This was a piece of cake. Although the *Benjamin Franklin* was a newer and more modern submarine than the *James Madison*, it wasn't that much different. I was able to complete my modified re-qual program in about three weeks without too much trouble. This left plenty of time for movies, card games, and anything else I wanted to do when not on duty.

There are a couple of stories that come to mind regarding this patrol. The first was a major casualty while we were transiting to our patrol area. Everything was normal and unassuming. My section was on watch, and I happened to be on the BQR-2B sonar equipment, listening to what was going on outside the boat. I had reported a sonar contact earlier during the watch and was tracking it. It was nothing but a cargo ship going its merry way, and of no concern.

Of the other two men in sonar, one was on break (Note: Each sonar watch stander would rest his ears after thirty minutes on the gear), and the other was operating the other sonar equipment. We were all pretty much at ease and talking off and on while doing our duties. All of a sudden, there was a tremendous *boom*, and the entire submarine experienced a *violent shake!* All three of us in sonar turned as white as a sheet and immediately concentrated on our jobs, as did the entire crew, I believe. Although it seemed to take forever, within a matter of seconds, everyone heard the voice of squatty body (that was his nickname), a short seasoned first-class submarine machinist mate, announced over the 4MC general announcing system, "Flooding in AMR 1, flooding in AMR 1!" AMR 1is auxiliary machine area number 1, which is located in the after part of the missile compartment. The missile compartment is about thirty-three feet wide, thirty-five feet high, and over one hundred ten feet long—about 35 percent of the entire boat. After hearing those words, I considered myself a dead man! I said a quick prayer, asking God to care of my wife and two boys and for me not to experience any pain. I then concentrated on doing my job. Just next to the BQR-2B, the sonar equipment I was operating, was located both a depth gauge and pit log (speed indicator) repeater. While making a careful sweep around (listening to everything around the submarine), my eyes were watching our depth and speed. After the careful sweep around, I contacted the Con with the following message: "Con Sonar, hold one contact, bearing 038 true, range five thousand yards, *clear to surface*!" Again, it seemed like an eternity before anything happened, but within another fifteen or twenty seconds, the entire submarine was at an upward angle with increased speed. Then after about fifteen more seconds, the boat leveled off at periscope depth just below the surface. Boy! What a feeling of relief, knowing we were no longer deep. At periscope depth, we should be able to overcome almost any flooding calamity. Well, to make a long story short, the cause of the large boom and violent shake was failure of a vacuum breaker valve on a waterline for our depth control tank system. The valve failure allowed water from the depth control tank to enter the people area of the submarine. Hence, the submarine was not taking on any outside ocean water. Of course, at the time, no one knew that! Squatty body, with the help of another crew member, was able to secure the piping and replace the valve. Along with me, many a crew member will never forget that experience. Additionally, I was told not to call out on the sonar/con announcing system clear to surface. ☺ Someone in control may think it an order from the office of the deck.

The second story was when we picked up a whiskey-class submarine (a whiskey-class submarine is a Russian-built diesel-powered submarine), making this either a Russian or Communist Chinese submarine. (Russia had sold many whiskeys to Communist China.) I do not recall which sonar section was on duty when the whiskey was contacted. However, the crew went to battle stations torpedo to ensure we would be prepared for the unexpected!

Russian whiskey-class submarine

The whiskey didn't have a clue we were tracking her. She was snorkeling and making all sorts of noise.

When a diesel-powered submarine snorkels, it is running its diesel engines underwater by raising a snorkel mast out of the water to allow air in for the engines and crew. This is done to recharge the batteries and yet stay submerged, except for the snorkel mast, which is next to impossible to see or pick up on radar.

She must have been on her way home, as she was not performing any evasive maneuvers. We tracked the whiskey all night, about eight hours. Mr. Holmberg, the commanding officer (CO), and the division officer were in and out of sonar all night. After about six hours, I finally asked Mr. Holmberg why we did not fire a torpedo at the whiskey. We had her cold! He explained that we were in international waters and we were not at war with the Russians or the Communist Chinese. I then asked why we were at battle stations torpedo. He stated that it was for practice and to ensure the whiskey didn't do anything that may cause us harm. I felt that had the situation been reversed, they would have fired at us. I was very young then and didn't know any better. About thirty minutes before sunrise, the whiskey stopped snorkeling and went deep and continued on her way. We tracked her for about another half hour and let her go as we went on our way. It was an exciting night and one I will not forget!

As with all patrols, this patrol came to its conclusion the first part of November. All that was left was to provide our counterparts on the gold crew with all the necessary information and be relieved, so we could fly home. As said earlier, changeover usually takes about four days total. Therefore, we were put into port routine. My in-port duty tasks were to assist in transferring all documents and equipment to our counterparts and standing a four-hour topside quarterdeck watch when our section had duty. Our section had duty the first full day in port, and I was assigned the 08:00–12:00 quarterdeck watch. It should be noted, during this time missile submarines had a quarterdeck watch armed with a .45-caliber semiautomatic pistol and a rover armed with an automatic carbine rifle.

The rover's job was to walk from the bow to the stern, checking both sides of the submarine, looking for anything abnormal, and to assist the quarterdeck watch as necessary. The quarterdeck watch was to ensure only authorized personnel came on the boat and record all events occurring every half hour or as needed. Most of the time, it was a rather mundane and boring job. However, there are times when it can be rather harrowing. This was one of those times!

It was about 09:30 when a man dressed as a lieutenant commander came aboard the boat. He was very cordial and seemed friendly. I began to get a little suspicious when he started questioning me about the patrol. He asked me what we did and a number of other things about which I was not authorized to talk about. When he realized I was not going to tell him anything, he said "Thank you" and started to walk to the hatch. I promptly asked him what he was doing and who he was. He told me his name and said he was the captain of the gold crew. This made me more suspicious. I had never seen a lieutenant commander as a captain of a missile submarine. All the commanding officers of missile boats I had seen were full commanders. I then asked to see his identification, so I could reference it to the authorized access list. He then told me he had left his ID on the tender. I said he would have to go back and get it. He then became somewhat testy and said he was going below. I said, *"No, you're not!"* I didn't know if I was being checked for my resilience or if he was a bad guy. Again, he said he was going below and started walking toward the hatch. I quickly drew my .45-caliber sidearm and jacked a round into the chamber while telling him to halt! Needless to say, when he heard the .45 jack a round into the chamber, he froze in his tracks. He began to tell me what to do, but I promptly told him to shut up and not to move, lest I would be forced to shoot him. I said I knew exactly what I needed to do.

With that, I got on the communication link between topside and below decks and demanded that proper authority come topside immediately. After a very short explanation of the last two minutes, proper authority came topside within one or two minutes. To my surprise, it was Mr. Holmberg, the XO, that came topside. Mr. Holmberg apparently knew the lieutenant commander and told me to put away my weapon and allow him to take the lieutenant commander under his charge. I replied, "Yes, sir," and entered the entire incident into the deck log and removed the .45 round from the chamber of my pistol.

Later that day, I was in sonar with my counterparts, performing changeover, when the captain, Mr. Holmberg, the lieutenant commander (LCDR), and the division officer all came into sonar. Mr. Holmberg smiled and asked me if I now knew the lieutenant commander. I said, "I do now," and smiled back. Then the lieutenant commander asked me if I would have really shot him. I told him with a straight face, "In a heartbeat!" He said, "Yes, I believe you would have." As they were all leaving, my division officer stopped and told me, "Well done! You made a lasting impression on the lieutenant commander, and the captain was pleased." Unfortunately, there was no official recognition for doing my job! Such is life!

Three days later, we were flying home, back to Pearl Harbor. I was anxious to see Derla and my sons. I could remember how much Freddy had changed while I was on deployments when on the *Madison* and was wondering how much little Robby had changed. I was really looking forward to being home and enjoying R&R. I was also a bit apprehensive about leaving the navy and looking for a job in the civilian world.

Being a submarine sonarman had its advantages. Aside from working in an air-conditioned space and a relatively comfortable environment, there are times when it is a very interesting job. When on patrol (deployment) in various parts of the world, there is nothing in the ocean around or near you except biologics. What are biologics, you ask? They are the numerous sounds created by the various creatures in the ocean. Whales, porpoises, shrimp, etc.—all make sounds! The particular sound I was most impressed with was that of the killer whale (orca). The loud screeching of the killer whale is so intimidating it will make all the other sounds in the area become completely quiet. It is absolutely incredible! One of my counterparts, stationed on another submarine, told me they were in an area with a very large amount of biologic activity. They decided to try an experiment with a killer whale recording they had. They piped the recording through the UQC (underwater telephone), and lo and behold, the entire area became extremely quiet! Whether this story is true, I can't say. However, I have no reason not to believe him.

I look back on all the times I have been at sea and believe I have been blessed to have seen and done all the things I have been exposed to. To be sure, there have been those times I have had the bejesus scared out of me and have had to work extremely hard in unpleasant conditions and surroundings. I think it safe to say that I spent about a year of my life underwater; nevertheless, I wouldn't trade the experience for the world!

Being home with Derla and the boys was great and rewarding. I began enjoying my R&R and working on my resume. At the beginning of the third week of my R&R, one of my sonarman shipmates told me to go to the new class he was assigned to attend. It was going to cover transistor and solid-state electronics. I reminded him I was being discharged from the active duty in January and I would *never* be given orders to such a school. He suggested I talk to the instructor and ask if I could audit the class, because our boat could only send one sonarman to the class. To my surprise, the instructor said he was okay with my auditing the class, provided I had a set of no-cost orders. This was not a problem. I went to Mr. Holmberg and asked if he would instruct the yeoman to type me a set of no-cost orders, so my location could be accounted for. Mr. Holmberg was okay with it, as I was still on R&R, using my own time, and was not needed for anything. As it turned out, this was an excellent two-week course. The two weeks were eight hours per day, which is more than a full three-semester hour course at the local college. This was excellent! It taught me transistors, integrated circuits, and solid-state technology. Needless to say, the instructor was very mad when he found out I had less than three weeks of active navy duty left. A minimum of two years of active service remaining was required to take this course. Boy, did I get lucky! Remember my dad. "Learn the system and make the system work for you."

The remaining three weeks went by very fast. Derla and I were busy getting all our things together for transfer to Long Beach, California, where I was to be given an honorable discharge from active service in the navy. This really had me very apprehensive and scared! For about the last eight years, all I knew was navy life and submarines. To leave this and become a civilian was totally foreign to me. Therefore, I called my parents, who were living in San Bernardino, California, at the time, and asked if we could stay with them for a little while until I had a job and got settled. Fortunately, they said yes.

Additionally, during those last three weeks in the navy, I was sending out resumes and answering wanted ads of every company that needed electronic technicians. You must remember, I was a submarine sonarman. Sonarmen not only operate the sonar equipment, they also maintain it and have the equivalent of an associate degree in electronics.

Off to San Bernardino and Civilian Life

In January of 1970, we arrived in California. Derla, Freddy, and Robby stayed with my mom and dad while I was in Long Beach, California, for about three days, being given an honorable discharge. Shortly after my honorable discharge, I had an interview with RCA, data processing department, in Los Angeles. As part of the interview, I was given an electronics test and scored rather high. God smiled on me! The test had numerous questions that were all covered in the two-week transistor and solid-state electronics course I had just finished three weeks earlier. RCA offered me a position as a CSR (customer service representative). This position required an initial thirteen-week training course in Cherry Hill, New Jersey. Boy, what a bummer! Once again, I was to be separated from Derla and my boys. At least this time I could write and receive letters and make phone calls. Also, the company would send me home for two long weekends during the training. This also dictated that Derla and I find an apartment, so we would not wear out our welcome with my mom and dad. The apartment wasn't very big. It was a little two-bedroom about two or three miles from Mom and Dad. After all, I wanted Derla to be close to my folks while I was away for training.

The training was somewhat difficult! Although I was reasonably well versed in electronics, I knew nothing about computers, digital logic, and the hexadecimal numbering system. This proved to be a real challenge. As it was in sonar school, I was sent to the board to decide whether to send me home or give me a two-week setback. Again, God smiled on me! The board decided to give me the setback, turning my thirteen weeks of training into fifteen weeks of training.

After training, I went back to San Bernardino and was to begin servicing RCA mainframe computer systems as part of a team of other CSRs. Also, Derla and I decided to look for a house. We decided to look in the north Long Beach area of the LA basin; this would keep me near my work sites while getting out of LA. Our first house was just a little two-bedroom, one-bath with a large detached two-car garage in what we thought was a pretty nice part of town.

It had now been about three months since my navy discharge. I missed the navy, and I did not like the thought of giving up about eight years of naval (military) service. After all, only twelve more years and I would have twenty years of military duty, making me eligible for military retirement. Therefore, I decided to check out the naval reserve program. That was one of the best decisions I have ever made. The naval reserves only required one weekend a month for training and two weeks a year for annual active duty training. It didn't take long for me to realize I liked being in the reserves. I got to play sailor, get paid for it, and was never away from home for more than two to three weeks at a time. Additionally, I was able to continue in my advancement. Although I was discharged from active duty for about three months, I was allowed to take the first-class advancement exam. I passed with flying colors and was promoted to STS1 (SS). This made my weekends more profitable. Military reserves are paid for their weekend training at the rate of one day's pay for every drill period, which is four hours.

About three months later, my supervisor called me into the office and informed me I was to be going to Dayton, New Jersey, for training on RCA video comp systems. It seems there was a shakeup in the organization, and my supervisor was given responsibility for the video comp systems in the LA basin and no longer had computer systems. This worked out pretty good for me in that I was no longer on probation (probation was ninety days as a new hire) and would receive more per diem while in training. However, I would be separated from Derla and the boys for about ten weeks, with two trips home. The training this time went much easier. I really didn't have to learn anything new other than the video comp system. The video comp system was electronic photo composition, which was a new and growing field.

I felt like I was on top of the world! I was doing well in the naval reserves and was doing well at RCA data processing. I owned a home (well, the mortgage company and me), had a great family, and life seemed good. I decided to do what I should have done while on shore duty in Pearl Harbor—go to college and get a degree. I thought I would first get an associate degree and then a bachelor's degree. So, I enrolled at Long Beach City College.

During the summer of 1971, I went on my first naval active duty for training at the submarine group in San Francisco. This proved to be a great assignment. There was not too much work to do, and the navy had a *self-help* program in place. This is where naval personnel could be used to do improvements in the facility, and the military only had to pay for the materials, as the personnel were already being paid by the government. It seems the commodore wanted to modify his office and conference area and asked for a couple of volunteers with electrical and carpentry skills. Another sailor with excellent carpentry skills and I took on the task. This was great duty. We did not have to stand any watches and pretty much kept our own hours. In a nutshell, we remolded his office and conference room with cabinets, drawers, and electrical outlets, and really made the entire area look great and function well. Both he and I were awarded a letter of appreciation for our excellent work, which also went back to our respective commands. Needless to say, this was another feather in my cap. As I said, I thought I was on top of the world. It didn't take too long for me to come back to earth.

Being a father, husband, homeowner, and going to school began to take its toll. Children cost money, homes cost money, and food costs money. I soon realized going to school had another function—it could provide me with extra income. I was eligible for the GI bill, and RCA would also reimburse me for my educational expenses. Believe it or not, this was better than getting a part-time job. However, it did mean I was away from home on school nights.

After about a year, things changed. RCA was undergoing a financial hardship and decided to sell off the data processing division. Boy, this was quite a shock. To lower the price of the division, there was a massive layoff. I had less than two years of service and was one of many that were let go.

Derla and I were extremely worried. I had never experienced anything like this. I decided to check the wanted ads to see if I could find another job. Also, I considered going back in the navy on active duty. Once again, the Lord was watching out for us. I located another position within a week. This position was working for Gerber Scientific Instrument Company. I was initially sent to Connecticut for about five weeks of training on their large computerized plotting tables. These tables were computer-controlled, high-precision plotting tools. Having had all the computer training at RCA made Gerber's training rather easy. After my training, I was assigned as the onsite representative at North American Rockwell, the company building the B-1 bomber, in the Los Angeles area. During the twelve to thirteen months I was with Gerber Scientific Instrument, I received calls from almost everyone, or so it seemed. It appears RCA released my name and I guess the others that were laid off out to the industry. I was happy at Gerber and did not respond to most of the inquirers.

Then I received an offer from Raytheon Service Company. It appeared they were not only interested in my technical experience, but they also wanted my submarine sonar experience. The division of Raytheon that wanted me had just received a large navy contract to retrofit the sonar on missile submarines. Needless to say, Raytheon made me an offer I *should* have refused. The pay was almost 15 percent more; however, it meant moving to Norfolk, Virginia. Raytheon really made it all sound great. They would pay us per diem while traveling and pay for the entire move to Norfolk. Before taking the position, I requested a formal offertory letter for protection. Upon receipt of the letter, I tendered my resignation with Gerber Scientific and took the job. We sold our house in Long Beach and headed for Norfolk. *Rats.* Was I in for a big surprise. The first few weeks on the job seemed okay. We bought another house in Virginia Beach, a suburb of Norfolk, and started to settle in. Then the reality of the job settled in. I was traveling almost constantly. I was away from home on various assignments for almost six months during my eight months with Raytheon. As if this was not bad enough, I was working for an absolute ungrateful, self-centered, aloof individual. I started looking for another position after only four months of being on the job with Raytheon.

I have to relate a specific story to illustrate what a buffoon my boss was. To begin with, I was still in the naval reserves. As a naval reservist, I always kept my supervisors apprised of my naval drill requirements. I would provide them with a memo listing all my drill dates for the next twelve months. I also added a couple of sentences explaining that I could change my drill dates if given adequate notice of about two weeks. Our retrofit group was comprised of about ten people, which were divided into two five-man teams.

We would work twelve-hour shifts. This group was sent to Holy Loch, Scotland, to perform a sonar retrofit on a missile submarine getting ready for deployment. It would take about three weeks. It was known in advance that three of the team members were to go to Rota, Spain, at the end of the retrofit to perform a pre-retrofit inspection on another missile submarine operating out of Rota. The day before I was to fly back to Norfolk, the team leader told me I was to take the five hundred dollars (that was a lot of money in 1972) advance given to one of the originally assigned persons and go to Rota in his place. This would cause me to miss my reserve drill meeting scheduled for the next weekend. Therefore, I immediately called the boss in Norfolk and informed him to reread the memo I provided and that I would have to fly back to Norfolk in time to make my drill. Although he was very upset, he told me to come home as originally scheduled, and the other person would go as it had been originally planned. I have no idea why my boss would do something so illogical, but this was a very common action in his management.

After arriving in Norfolk, my boss called me into the office and told me I had mixed loyalties. I should always put Raytheon first. I told him that was a very strange way to feel because it was the navy contract that was paying all our salaries! I was so upset that same afternoon I went to Congressman Whitehurst's Norfolk office and obtained a copy of the Sailors' and Soldiers' Relief Act. This act required civilian companies to allow their military reservist time off to perform their drills. The congressman's secretary also informed me that the company refusing to allow a reservist to drill could lose any and all military contracts. The next day, I went into my boss's office and slammed the copy of the act on his desk. He became quite concerned and asked me what I told them at the congressman's office. I told him that I said only what was needed, but if he messed with me again, I would go back and tell the congressman everything. Needless to say, the relationship between me and my boss got much worse. That was okay; I had already accepted a position with Texas Instruments and was being transferred to Dallas, Texas.

It was a few weeks earlier that I had an interview with TI. I saw an ad in the Norfolk newspaper for technicians wanted at Texas Instruments. I answered the ad and dropped off my resume. The actual interview did not go very well. You see, I was expecting an interview and was told it would last about an hour. In reality, it would have taken about two or three hours. They wanted me to fill out an application and many other forms. That in itself was not so bad; however, I was then given a test that required the use of a slide rule (this was before the day of the calculator) and another hour or so. I had just returned home from a trip and had promised Derla I would take her to dinner that evening. We had a babysitter lined up and reservations for a specific time. This did not leave me enough time to do everything the TI reps wanted and still interview. I decided to tell the TI reps they misled me by saying the entire interview would only last an hour. I was gainfully employed and had a dinner engagement that I was not going to miss. I gave them a copy of my resume and left. During dinner, I told Derla I was not going to be working with Texas Instruments.

To my surprise, a couple of weeks later, while on another assignment in Portsmouth, Rhode Island, I received a call from a Mr. Jordan Lofye from TI. Mr. Lofye had called our house wanting to talk to me, and Derla had given him my hotel phone number in Portsmouth. Mr. Lofye asked if I would come to Dallas for an interview. I informed him I was on an assignment and would not be able to come to Dallas for at least three weeks. Mr. Lofye then asked if I would be willing to interview in Portsmouth if he came to Rhode Island. Naturally, I said yes. I surmised that there must be something in my resume that caught his eye. Sure enough, Mr. Lofye was in charge of the photo plotting group that was using Gerber Scientific Instrument equipment. It seems the TI technicians were not very accomplished at keeping the systems up and running. Having worked for Gerber made me somewhat valuable to Mr. Lofye's group.

Mr. Lofye and I had dinner and interviewed almost all evening. He was a great guy and had also been a sonarman on minesweepers while he was in the navy. We really hit it off very well. Upon leaving, he said he would have HR send me an offertory letter, and I could tender my resignation from Raytheon.

By June of 1973, we sold our house in Virginia Beach, Virginia, and moved to Richardson, Texas. We rented a house about two miles from the Texas Instruments site in

Dallas. This would allow us time to find a house that we wanted to buy. I also transferred my naval reserve affiliation to the Dallas area.

During the next three or four months, Derla and I were busy looking for a home. It seemed like we were looking at two or three homes every day after I got home from work. Boy, what a hassle! I told Derla I didn't want to look anymore. She should go and look while I was at work. If she saw one she liked, I would then go and see it after work. Finally, in October, she found a home we both liked and put a contract on it. We closed just before Christmas of 1973.

It was about six months or so, while in Richardson, that I read the book *The Richest Man in Babylon* by George S. Clason. This book changed the course of our financial lives. It taught me the importance of saving at least 10 percent of the money you make and being debt-free. It took us about twenty years before we were saving over 10 percent of our income and being almost debt-free. By the time I retired in 2003, I was saving almost 20 percent of my salary. Because of this book and a few others, Derla and I are able to have a quite comfortable retirement. See my booklet, *Investing in Real Estate the Wrong Way*, for a complete review of how we were able to have a happy retirement.

My first five years (1973 to 1978) at TI were great. I was able to complete my associate degree in digital electronics and begin work on my bachelor's program. Additionally, I was able to advance to chief petty officer in the navy. Life seemed good.

In 1974, Derla and I learned we were going to have another child. This was a bit of a surprise, as we didn't plan for it to happen. However, we were pleased. To our surprise, our daughter, Mahealani, was born on August 17, 1974.

Also, during this time, Derla decide to fulfill her lifelong desire to become a nurse. With a lot of hard work and study, she received her nursing license in 1977.

Then in the latter part of 1978, I learned my boss, Jorden Lofye, was being promoted to a better position. Naturally, I thought I would be promoted to his old position, as I had proven myself while Jorden was on vacation, in the hospital, and on convalescence for over five weeks. When I learned management wanted me to train who was to be my new supervisor, I became very upset and decided to leave TI.

For the next five years, I worked for two other companies that had me traveling all over the US. Although I made a pretty good income, I was not at home spending time with my children and continuing my education. *Boy*, what a mistake. Children need their father around! Fortunately, I continued to advance in the naval reserves. I was promoted to senior chief (E-8) in three years after making chief and got promoted to master chief (E-9) after only two and a half years of making senior chief. This was quite a surprise. It seems no one at the promotion board was paying much attention. You are supposed to be a senior chief for three years before you can be promoted to master chief. Once again, I got lucky. Yes, God had smiled on me again! I made master chief while only having eighteen years of both active and reserve duty. This is not the norm. Most persons promoted to master chief have between twenty to twenty-four years of service. Being promoted to master chief required me to attend a training course for all E-9s in New Orleans. The PM (personnel man), when reviewing my personal records, was beside himself. He said I had no business being a master chief, as I wasn't a senior chief for three years! I told him it was the selection board that promoted me to master chief and I wasn't going to give it back! Being a master chief made navy life *great*. I applied for and went on numerous special assignments needed by the navy.

By the Grace of God, I saw an opening at Texas Instruments that required my skills. I applied and was accepted back at TI; this allowed me to go back to school and complete my Bachelor of Science program. After I obtained my Bachelor of Science, TI promoted me to process engineer, working in the semiconductor manufacturing area. This lasted about another six years. Unfortunately, it was 1997, and there was a large downturn in the demand for the semiconductors TI was manufacturing; therefore, a large layoff occurred. Fortunately, I was successful in finding another position working in both photo lithography and wet/clean etch as a process engineer. I stayed in the semiconductor industry for about eight more years.

Conclusion

It was in September of 2003 that I decided to retire. I had been sent to Fishkill, New York, in June of 2002 and did not like it. New York and, for that matter, New Jersey and Massachusetts seem to have less-than-friendly inhabitants. For sure, after you get to know them, they are friendly, but not like Texas. I asked the company to send me back to Dallas but was told there were no openings. Not wanting to spend another winter in New York, I tendered my resignation. Having retired from the navy in 1993 and being eligible to begin drawing from my navy pension, I felt Derla and I would be in good shape. Additionally, I was given a part-time teaching position at Richland College. It was only a year or so later that I began my adventure in real estate. That adventure is another story in itself. Again, see my booklet *Investing in Real Estate the Wrong Way*!

Not only has my life as a civilian been good, but staying in the naval reserves also had its rewards. I have been able to stay associated with submarines and even go out to sea. Most of my active naval reserve assignments have been at MOTU billets. MOTU is a mobile technical unit. The job of MOTU personnel is to assist and teach naval personnel assigned to fleet units to correct and repair problems with the highly technical electronic equipment on today's ships and submarines. Being an engineer made performing my naval reserve assignments at MOTU units somewhat easy. Needless to say, I have been on numerous submarines and other ships, repairing and assisting shipboard personnel in the maintenance of their equipment. This has been extremely rewarding. Additionally, I was privileged to serve on three promotion boards and one high year tenure board at the Naval Annex next to the Pentagon. Over the twenty-three years in the naval reserves, I had the privilege to be assigned to bases in San Diego, California; Norfolk, Virginia; Pearl Harbor, Hawaii; Subic Bay in the Philippines; and even NAS Dallas in Grand Prairie, Texas. On many of these assignments, Derla would accompany me. This afforded us the opportunity to continue our travels around the world.

On another assignment to MOTU in the Philippines, I accompanied a chief ET, on shore duty at the Subic MOTU, to a large ship moored in the harbor. That ship had two problems reported. One was sonar, and the other was a fathometer (UQN) problem. Not being familiar with the type of sonar on that ship, I told the chief I would tackle the fathometer. On the bridge, where the fathometer was located, I questioned the quartermaster technician (QM) on duty what the problem was. After he related the systems, I become somewhat excited. I had the exact same problem on one of the submarines I had worked on. I ask the QM to fetch me the tools I would need and a cup of coffee so we could resolve this situation report. After about two hours of total time, the fathometer was up and running perfectly. When the chief came to get me, he was quite surprised the problem was resolved. That problem had been on the to-do board for about a week. I had to confess I had that same problem a few years back on another submarine. He said he didn't care; it was one less problem on the to-do board.

During this trip, about eight of our group decided to go to the island of Corregidor. To my surprise, they decided to go in *bangkas*—basically, a dugout canoe with a lawn mower motor for propulsion. Going to the island wasn't too bad. However, the trip back was very harrowing. We were on Corregidor for about four hours, visiting World War II sites. I must say, seeing the Malinta Tunnel was quite impressive. It was so large it even had a large hospital in it! During those four hours, the weather got rather bad. After only ten minutes in the *bangka*, the only time I could see land was when we crested a wave. I was very concerned about being swapped and having to swim to shore. That in itself was not my worry. I could swim for a long time. I feared being eaten by a shark! On our way back to the naval base we decided to take the scenic route. This would allow us to see the country side and let our cloth dry. Along the way there were little kiosk every five to ten miles. They were about ten by twelve Little Shacks that sold beer, soda, and a number of other things the locals could use. At one such stop there were a few young children present; so I bought some candy and passed it to the youngsters. Before I finished my beer there must have been at least twenty children present. I ask the lady in charge if the large gallon and a half bowl on the counter was candy. She said yes, so I took the bowl and started handing out candy to all the kids. The lady (owner) got very concerned and bewildered. I told her not to worry, I would pay for it. After the bowl was empty I asked what I owed. She got her calculator and tallied it up. Wow! I owed about five dollars. A cheap price to pay to give a little happiness to those less fortunate. Looking back on the adventure, I do have fond memories.

On the beach, waiting for the bangkas

getting in the bangka

On my last assignment to Subic Bay, I suggested that Derla come over to visit me. This would give her a chance to see one of the places I was stationed while on my active naval duty assignments. I had arranged for Derla to go shopping with the wife of my counterpart there at Subic. His wife was a Filipina and could take Derla all over the place. Derla, being Hawaiian Chinese, could easily pass for being Filipina. Being a Filipina, she would be able to get very good prices buying local Philippine goods. When they got back to the base, Derla had spent over three hundred dollars. That amounts to over six thousand Philippine pesos. Keep in mind that the average wage for a Philippine worker was about twenty-five pesos per day back then. We shipped back seven boxes of wood-carved jewelry boxes, wood-carved salad bowl sets, wood carvings, table cloths, and many other Philippine-made goods. These seven boxes were about two feet by two feet by four feet. Naturally, there was lots of packing material to keep all the items secure. We had gifts for Christmas, birthdays, weddings, and almost any other occasion for the next three years! Additionally, we took an extra week for vacation so we could visit Japan on our way back to the States. In Japan, we visited Tokyo, Kyoto, and many other places, the names I do not recall. I do remember visiting a place that housed a *giant* Buddha. I was truly impressed! This Buddha was made in the seventeenth century. I cannot imagine how they built it! In Kyoto, we visited the castle that was featured in the TV series *Shogun*. Again, I was very impressed. This castle was over four hundred years old and even had an alarm system in the sleeping quarters of the shogun and his family.

Another story I would like to share: was my assignment during Desert Storm in December of 1991. I was called to active duty and sent to Pearl Harbor. When I checked in, I was informed the chief's quarters were under renovation. Therefore, the assignment clerk said for me to find a hotel in which to stay. Being in a hotel necessitated having a rent-a-car and receiving per diem. As almost all the ships were sent to the Gulf War area, there was nothing for me and the other few men assigned to the MOTU to do. Therefore, we were released about 11:00 each day. After the fourth day, I called Derla and told her to fly over and be with me, visit with her family, and help me enjoy my "vacation." Sometimes our military really knows how to waste money and resources.

Me in Pearl Harbor during Desert Storm.
December 1991.

Additionally, since being retired, I have accepted short-term engineering contracts ranging from ten days to seven months in duration. These contracts have been in France, Ireland, Japan, and here in the States. Derla would accompany me on many of these contracts, allowing us to see even more of the world.

On one such assignment, I was sent to Paris, France, and Dublin, Ireland. This assignment was going to last between six months to a year. The assignments came with the company paying for my lodging, rent-a-car, and per diem. Therefore, once I was set up in a bed-and-breakfast, Derla came over to stay with me. My schedule was working twelve-hour shifts, three days on and four days off and four days on and three days off. Almost every time we had four days off, we would go somewhere. Having been provided with a rent-a-car, we drove all over Paris and went to the top of the Eiffel Tower. I have to say, Derla and I really did not like France very much. Although the countryside and the French Alps are beautiful, the French seem to be less than friendly, especially the Parisians! We even drove to Monte Carlo and spent a weekend there. Boy, if you do not own one of the yachts in the harbor, you have no business being there! That place is very expensive! We then flew to Rome and visited the city. While there, we took a trip to Naples and toured Pompeii. On our three days off, we drove all over Ireland, visiting tourist sights. When it would start to get dark, we would look for a bed-and-breakfast. The next morning, we would continue our sightseeing. After seven months, this assignment was over. We had a great time!

Derla and me with actors at the Roman Coliseum

Derla and me at the Trevi Fountain in Rome

Derla at the Blarney Castle in Ireland

I could tell many more stories of the short-term contracts and naval assignments I have had and the excitement these assignments have allowed, in addition to the many sights Derla and I have been able to see. However, I am fearful it would appear as though I were bragging.

Bragging or not, I feel there is one more story I wish to tell. It was while assigned to the submarine base on Point Loma in San Diego as part of the MOTU detachment. There were three of us assigned there because we were all qualified-on submarines—Master Chief Rich Ost, an ET (electronics technician); Chief Devern Austin, also an ET; and myself, a master chief sonarman. As mentioned earlier, MOTU personnel are to assist and teach shipboard personnel on the maintenance of their equipment. It was about 16:00, and Ost (Master Chief Ost) and I were at the Point Loma MOTU facility, waiting to go back to the assigned quarters to get ready to go to the club. It was Friday, and the chief's club was to have some topped named entertainment we all wanted to see. Being concerned about Chief Austin, Ost and I decided to go to the boat he was assigned to work on. The boat was a nuc fast attack and was due to deploy in a few days. When we arrived on board, we found Devern up to his ears in alligators, working on the navigation equipment. So, Ost and I dove in to help him. After about an hour, we had narrowed the problem to a signal transmission line in one of the equipment cabinets noted on the schematics. I asked the crew member working with us where the cabinet in question was. After he pointed it out, I told him and one of the other crew members to open it up. Once open, I grabbed a flashlight and climbed in. With Devern and Ost at the schematic hollering out the wire connection designators, I began looking at all the connection panels. To be sure, the wire carrying the missing signal was broken from the connector. Ost handed me a new wire connector and a screwdriver. One of the crew members held the flashlight for me so I could make the repair. After the crew buttoned everything up, we all tested the system to ensure proper operation. With this problem report solved, MOTU had another feather in its cap, and the reserve component attached to MOTU got a feather in its cap. The active MOTUs at Subic Bay, Pearl Harbor, and San Diego all welcomed our reserve detachment to come for assignment. *We got things done!* As I said, we were all either engineers or advanced technicians.

All in all, we have had a great life! I have been married to a wonderful woman for over fifty-three years; have three grown children, eight grandchildren, and two great-grandchildren. I have fulfilled my dream of serving on submarines and becoming an engineer. Derla and I have truly got it made! We have been to over twenty-eight countries, twenty islands, forty-six of the fifty states, and five of the seven continents. God has truly blessed us, especially me!

As I mention in my booklet *Investing in Real Estate the Wrong Way*, Derla and I plan to sell the remaining rental properties we own; with those proceeds, we plan to truly enjoy whatever remaining years our Gracious Lord will allow us to have.

Printed in the United States
By Bookmasters